THE ARMCHAIR GUIDE TO PROPERTY INVESTING

How to retire on $2,000 a week

Ben Kingsley and Bryce Holdaway

First published in 2016 by Major Street Publishing Pty Ltd.
Contact: info@majorstreet.com.au or phone: 0421 707 983

National Library of Australia Cataloguing-in-Publication entry:
Creator: Kingsley, Ben, author.
Title: The armchair guide to property investing: how to retire on
$2,000 a week/Ben Kingsley and Bryce Holdaway.
ISBN: 9780994256041 (paperback)
Notes: Includes index.
Subjects: Real estate investment – Australia.
Investment – Australia.
Retirement – Australia – Planning.
Retirement income – Australia.
Finance, Personal – Australia.
Other Creators/Contributors:
Holdaway, Bryce, author.
Dewey Number: 332.632430994

ISBN: 978-0-9942560-4-1

Internal design by Production Works
Cover design by Anis Riana, 9 green studio
Cover photo by Beth Jennings Photography
Bryce and Ben are dressed by Menzclub, www.menzclub.com.au
Printed in Australia by Griffin Press

10 9 8 7 6 5 4 3 2

Acknowledgments

We would like to thank Annie Reid from Atrium Media (www.atrium.media) for her patience, guidance and overall support throughout the writing of the manuscript.

We would also like to acknowledge all those professionals who have come before us, who have been generous of their time in sharing their own knowledge and experience to allow us to continue our work and crusade in helping others with their property, finance and wealth creation.

Dedications

To my mum and dad who showed me the world, taught me the benefits of hard work and who gave me a wonderful moral compass and desire for helping others.

To my wife, Jane, who supports me unconditionally and allows me the time to follow my passions, whilst being the best mother ever to our two beautiful boys – Jack and Harry.

I love you all,

BEN

To my wonderful parents, Graham and Christine, thank you for instilling in me a sense of the importance of family, hard work and empathy for others, while offering me opportunities in life that you both worked so hard to afford me.

To my sister, Lisa, thanks for being my constant best friend and for your never-ending encouragement on the end of the phone, no matter whether I'm up or down.

To my beautiful wife Andrea, thank you for selflessly encouraging me to chase my ambition and to experience the 'road less travelled', while offering unconditional nurturing and mentoring to our amazing boys, Jack and Samuel.

BRYCE

To Michael Pope and Michael Savy. Your knowledge and experience is also spread throughout these pages. It's an absolute privilege to have you both as our business partners and of great comfort to know that we are able to draw on your wisdom when called upon.

To the Empower Wealth team. Quite simply, without your commitment and dedication we could not help the number of people that we do. You are a credit to yourselves and we are blessed to be able to work alongside you all.

BEN & BRYCE

CONTENTS

PREFACE:
THE TRUTH WILL SET YOU FREE

Do you often find yourself daydreaming about how great life would be if you had enough money to do what you wanted to do? Where you wouldn't have to worry about what was in the bank and whether it would be enough for now and for your future needs? And, finally, you didn't have to actively go to work anymore to generate an income?

Have you ever allowed yourself to dream of having free time to take those regular overseas holidays each year, spend more time connecting with family and friends, or being in a financial position to give your kids the best education and learning opportunities? Or what about being able to afford the best health care if things don't go as planned, pursuing your hobbies with passion and time, or simply spending your retirement without a worry in the world?

Taking that concept a little further, imagine having $2,000 a week to spend for life! And guess what – the kicker is that it should only require an investment of 10 hours of your time per property per year. That's right; per year, a little over a full day's work to manage each property within your property portfolio that can generate a passive income for that lifestyle you've always wanted.

You'll be able to sleep at night, rest easy and be safe in the knowledge that you can enjoy what you've worked for over your whole life. Let's put it another way – in today's money $2,000 a week is the equivalent of living off $104,000 each year, which would also put you in one of the highest brackets of retirement earnings in the country.

Sounds fantastic, doesn't it?

However, the Australian landscape currently paints a very different story of how our wealth is shaping up. Each year, more and more reports are released suggesting very few of us will have enough savings, superannuation and investments to comfortably retire on. Many will be forced to work longer in order to fund their retirement. It's really concerning and a fairly bleak picture, which is capitalised on by all forms of advertisements keen to get you to start acting more now in order to do less in the future.

How are these for some scary statistics: 20 per cent of our population own over 60 per cent of our private wealth and sadly the bottom 20 per cent of our population only own just 1 per cent of Australia's private wealth. The top 20 per cent control over 40 per cent of all income and the lowest earn just 7 per cent. It's very clear that the vast majority of Australians have no real idea about money, finance and investing. Their financial literacy and understanding is below where it needs to be. Those who are in the top 20 per cent are people who have mastered the concepts, theory, mindset, resources and overall knowledge of money, finance and investing. We'd also bet they have had and continue to have sound professional advisers guiding them and helping them plan, manage and take calculated risks to add to their wealth.

Unfortunately, making your money work harder for you and creating wealth is not easy; if it were, everyone would be rich and we'd all be laughing on the way to the bank. Yet wealth creation is a massive global industry. Today, thousands of spruikers, so-called 'educators or coaches', advertise get-rich-quick programs, offering 'secret formulas' or the 'one strategy that really works' to vulnerable and uneducated subscribers who happily fork out cash and expect instant life-changing results. Then there are the countless ways to control money, access finance, invest and implement different investment strategies, each covered off in the thousands of books that have been written over time.

Creating personal wealth through property investing is a multi-billion-dollar industry, but sadly, there is a lack of independent property advice and quality research that supports some investment decisions. These get-rich-quick schemes might sound great on stage at the promoters' seminars or in their slick video productions but on closer investigation they reveal massive shortcomings.

The most obvious shortcomings relate to them presenting and 'pushing' a strategy that doesn't take into account your own personal financial situation, your risk profile to investing, your investment and retirement timeframes. There is nothing offering a complete solution tailored to you and your circumstances. It's just 'cookie cutting' – these off-the-shelf sales pitches are far more likely to result in these spruikers getting rich than you! Think of it like this, the guys selling the mining tools generally end up making more money than those actually doing the mining. Don't even get us started on how they 'gloss over' all the detail that goes into investing in property.

Our motivation for writing this book is not one of documenting our own personal success as property investors, as many of these self-help style books do. Instead, our motivation stems from trying to stop individuals from getting fooled by these smooth-talking, well-scripted spruikers, by showing you how it's done when you work with true, qualified professional advisers, who choose this as a career.

Our 'armchair' approach is all about presenting the real facts, figures, theories, risks and strategies in a proven framework and process that's easy to read, easy to understand and, hopefully, even easier to implement into your life – just as if you were having a professional consultation with us.

We strongly believe that 'the truth will set you free'. We will dispel the myths, shut down the spruikers and demonstrate to you our fundamental philosophy – that every Australian can improve their financial position.

For us, it all boils down to quality and balanced information – the good, the bad and the ugly – because if you have the right tools, process and knowledge, you will be better prepared to make informed and calculated decisions. These decisions aren't based on hype or fear, or a one-size-fits-all approach. Our view is simply that without sound knowledge and a proven professional approach, you're flying blind.

We will cut through the noise in the money and wealth creation space by addressing the fundamental principles – foundation, theory and action – which we all should learn and fully understand. Your understanding of and competency in this information is the knowledge that should propel you on your journey to a vastly improved financial position over the long term. With the right education, you'll be able to much more effectively carve out a holistic, tailor-made solution to suit yours and your family's needs.

As qualified and experienced professionals in our fields, we know there are complex variables, assumptions and investment parameters which can be overwhelming for most just starting out. Yet in writing this book, we have adopted the 'KISS' (keep it simple, stupid) approach to keep it as easy as possible to understand. Just imagine that we're all having a chat over a coffee at your place, presenting some ideas and giving you our two-cents worth of what's worked for us and our clients that can just as equally work for you. If our hundreds of clients can understand it and benefit from it, then hopefully you can too!

Finally, before you start this book and your potential new pathway to improved wealth, we want to congratulate you for allocating time out of your busy life to invest in yourself and your potential to be what you want to be. We hope this book contributes in a positive way to your journey of discovery and eventual fulfilment.

BEN & BRYCE
Melbourne, 2016

THE AUTHORS' STORIES

Ben Kingsley

CEO & Founder, Empower Wealth
Co-host of The Property Couch podcast
Chair, Property Investment Professionals of Australia (PIPA)
Qualified Property Investor Adviser (QPIA)
Diploma of Finance and Mortgage Broking Management
Diploma of Business
Property Investment Analyst
Buyers' Agent – Licensed Real Estate Agent (VIC, NSW, QLD & SA)

My story's not one of those rags-to-riches clichés that you read about. You know the ones – I was down to my last $10 or I was working as a 'shelf-stacker' before I made my millions. Personally, I had 'no down on my luck' story before I made it big! My journey has taught me more about working smarter, not harder.

I was born in Melbourne and grew up in the early 1970s in the northern suburb of Bundoora – pretty much a middle/working class area on the city fringe back then. I grew up in a great neighbourhood with lots of other kids who played footy, basketball and cricket in the large court where our house was situated.

From the age of about 13, I realised my cup of tea was commerce. My dad was an aircraft engineer with Ansett and he was the treasurer of the Ansett basketball club. For most of my youth there were plenty of fundraisers held at our house (the unofficial clubrooms), after which, the next day, I remember helping dad count the money raised, record the figures in his ledger book and then finally take the money to the bank. I also remember my dad investing in shares and doing anything that would help our family create and build on our wealth base. As a result, it was logical that I was more attracted to commerce studies, such as accounting, economics and maths, than science or languages. So much was this the case that some of my classmates in my late high school years even referred to me as Alex P. Keating from 'Family Ties' (the US sitcom of the day) because of my outspoken interest in business, money and wealth-building!

I started investing in shares with my dad's help when I was 15 years old. The share market crash of 1987 came one year later, which taught me that not every investment is a winner every time. But it didn't totally deter me from the share market, as I still thought I could make more money on shares than putting the money in the bank over a five-year period. As it turned out, I was right when my share investments provided a better return. I sold them when I was 23 to help buy my first property in late 1994.

My first mistake

At 23, I knew very little about residential property. I knew that buying my own house had far more to do with having my own freedom and space than with investing. In my naivety, I did what most first-timers do – I bought a property in the same suburb I grew up in, Bundoora. In fact, it was actually across the road in the same court where my folks lived. So much for freedom and my own space, but the odd free meal and use of the old man's lawn mower and mum's willingness to do the occasional load of washing was very handy indeed!

This first property grew at a rate of over 5 per cent p.a. over the next six years, so technically I wasn't really making any great gains out of it. In the meantime, I had moved interstate to pursue a career in the tourism industry. Having grown up with a dad working in the airline industry, we enjoyed the benefits of cheap flights and from this my other passion of travel was born. Being able to combine a business career with travel was perfect for me at that time.

My second mistake

In 2000, I met an accountant whom I had been referred to, in Sydney. He advised me to sell my Melbourne property (in October 2000) and buy a property in the Sydney market instead. He said the property in Melbourne was now cash flow positive and I was paying too much tax. As this particular tax professional had several investment properties himself, I thought he knew what he was doing, so I took his advice and sold the property.

That was my second dumb mistake. I took this accountant's tax-saving advice rather than getting more holistic advice that incorporated my overall wealth-building perspective. With the benefit of hindsight, and now given my own professional qualifications, I realised he didn't think outside of the tax box to see other possible ways to achieve a superior wealth outcome. A better solution would have been to hold on to the Melbourne property, renovate the kitchen and bathroom, then release the increased equity to enable me to secure a second property in the Sydney market.

To date, that decision to sell the Bundoora property has cost me more than $365,000 in lost wealth. By the time I retire at the age of 50, (I'm 44 now) it will be more like $500,000 and counting. So you can see why I want to prevent others from making these types of mistakes – hundreds of thousands of dollars lost!

Using the cash from the Melbourne home sale, I spent the next six months doing on-the-ground research before securing a property in Sydney. I was far better researched this time, spending hundreds of hours attending open houses (about 20 each weekend), auctions, reading books, magazines, local newspapers, recording sales (remember this was the early days of the internet with limited access to property data), as well as attending seminars and expos. Jane (my future wife) and I bought a single-fronted, semi-detached property in Alexandria – about 4 km from Sydney's CBD. We bought it for $395,000 in March 2001. Straightaway, it was a winner and within two years it was valued at over $550,000. At the time of publishing this book, it's valued at over $1 million.

The next phase in my journey

I had a great career in tourism, working my way up to national sales manager for Australia and New Zealand for Hamilton Island Resort and then national sales and marketing manager for Australia and New Zealand for Voyages Hotels and Resorts – namely Ayers Rock Resort and others. Given that I'd worked for the two biggest resorts in Australia, I had a decision to make; take my career overseas to work in other large, integrated resorts or look for a new career opportunity. (I didn't want to just work in a nice hotel – boring!) I was now engaged to Jane and my work involved spending a lot of time travelling. There wouldn't be a fortnight when I wasn't spending some time on a plane away from Jane.

We decided it was time to move back to Melbourne as we were about to get married. By this stage in my life, I knew the things I was passionate about – property investing, money, wealth-building, business and engaging with people, whether it be helping others or collaborating with colleagues. I was ready to start my own business and build a property and wealth advisory practice.

It was time to hit the books and study to become the best adviser I could be. This meant acquiring a greater understanding of the finance component of property investing. So I completed my qualifications as a mortgage broker and bought a Mortgage Choice franchise. It's one thing to have a qualification, but what better way to learn the skills and gain the experience I needed to help others than to jump in at the deep end and use the resources available to me within a franchise network.

In 2007, I decided to exit Mortgage Choice and start up an independent business so I could realise my true dream of setting up a holistic property and wealth advisory company. This was the beginnings of Empower Wealth, a fully-integrated wealth advisory practice with a team of specialist advisers.

My business dream

Since opening our doors back in 2007, I have realised the first stage of my business vision. Empower Wealth has more than 20 staff and we provide specialist property investment advice, buyers agency, property research, financial planning and money management services. We service over 2,000 clients as they strive to achieve financial freedom. Nationally we are recognised as one of Australia's leading property investment advisory companies.

The second stage of my dream (that Bryce also shares) is to better educate more Australians about property investing and striving to achieve a self-funded retirement. In early 2015, we launched a free weekly podcast called 'The Property Couch'. It has become the most popular investment podcast in Australia and its only purpose is to educate listeners on smart property investing. In addition to this podcast, we have written hundreds of articles, presented to thousands of people, produced over a hundred educational videos and been interviewed by a range of TV and print media. This is all with the clear goal of better educating consumers to make smarter property investment decisions.

Along the way, Empower Wealth has been a finalist and won many awards in the residential property industry, which speaks volumes for the dedicated team of people who work with us, and their focus on giving the best advice to help households achieve financial freedom. I have also been fortunate to have won the only recognised national award for property investment advisers – the *Your Investment Property* Magazine Property Investment Adviser of the Year in 2014 and 2015.

Personally, since returning to Melbourne, Jane and I have been able to buy several more investment properties to build up a multi-million-dollar property investment portfolio for ourselves and now our two boys. I use exactly the same principles, follow the same frameworks and processes, and build the same property investment plan myself that I do for my clients and which we showcase in this important book.

Our personal plan has the target of generating a passive income of $160,000 a year by the time I am 50. Using the same information in this book, my wife and I have been able to execute our plan to become financially independent and buy quality investment properties that are producing great results. We are on top of our money management and we look forward to being able to have the choice of wanting to work versus having to work. Plus we will have more free time to enjoy our children and the things that interest us – especially travelling!

Why? What motivates me?

There are a few things that have motivated me in the past and new ones now that continue to motivate me to achieve a self-funded retirement.

The first couple of motivations come from my own upbringing and watching and adopting the money habits of my parents. My mum and dad worked really hard to provide for my brother and I, while also building their wealth in the same process. Like many households, striking the right balance between having money for today and putting money away for tomorrow resulted in some arguments about prioritising this money. Mum worked hard to stretch every dollar far enough to run the household, and dad focused on paying down the mortgage sooner and continuing to build the family's wealth base.

As I said earlier, mine is not a rags-to-riches story, we certainly didn't go without, but again it's that balancing act of 'keeping up with the Joneses' and living for today, and the opportunity cost of what happens if you spend it today and don't put enough away for building wealth for tomorrow.

So my first 'Why' motivation stems from my memories of when I was in my mid to late teens and Dad and Mum were always conscious of the state of the family budget. I thought if we had more money on top of what they were both working to generate, then money would no longer be a concern. I remember telling myself when I have my own place, and one day have a family, that my aim would be to create enough wealth and passive income to ensure that there was little reason to worry about money or to keep to a strict budget.

My second 'Why' motivation comes from watching my dad work three jobs for over 30 years, while mum worked part-time and brought up two boys, so that they could be in a position to retire at the age of 55. Their effort showed me that it's possible to retire earlier if you sacrifice most of your leisure time to generate a greater income, but it came at the personal cost of having less time to spend with the family.

To their absolute credit, my parents' hard work paid off and they did retire at 55. They live a great life now and don't really want for anything. They have been retired for over 14 years and are still going strong. Seeing them have the freedom they enjoy and the fact they may have the financial stability for another 30-plus years of retirement justifies their efforts.

However, as I developed my understanding of money and investing I realised that if you invest wisely, you can potentially reduce the need to earn more income, as the money you have invested does the heavy lifting, instead of you doing it. So my second motivation was that I didn't want to have to work three jobs to make my future look bright. I wanted to learn how to invest smartly and have those investments give me the income returns and compound in value to provide me with passive income, so that I wouldn't need to work extra jobs or hours to generate that income.

To do this I needed to become knowledgeable about all things investing. That's what took me on the journey of educating myself, both on a personal and then ultimately on a professional level, to have the intelligence and tools to make smarter investment decisions.

My next 'Why' motivation has evolved from outside the family experiences. It actually stems from my exposure to a combination of things. First, as you embark on this knowledge-building journey, especially in the property investment area, you will come across property spruikers. Early in my journey I saw plenty of them at many a seminar or event, and what shocked me the most was not so much the spruikers themselves but how so many audience members 'bought' their sales pitch and were seduced into signing up.

When I became qualified in lending and property investment, and then experienced in advising households on managing their money, it hit home just how little people knew about money or investing and how easily they can be misled. They can seriously jeopardise their wealth prospects by either putting their heads in the sand, because they are taking advice from anyone other than someone formally qualified to give it, or taking the advice of a spruiker, which has already or will cause a great amount of financial pain. Don't be fooled by those who claim to be educators or coaches but don't have any formal qualifications or who aren't willing to put their so-called investment recommendations into a formal written plan!

I absolutely love what I do now and I honestly believe that every household has the potential to improve their financial position through better money management, better planning and better investment execution. Unfortunately most households don't know how, and this is yet another 'why' reason, the desire to 'pay it forward'. Property investment has been very good to me personally and I want others to be in a position to enjoy the results of investing in property as I have done. I spend my working day doing exactly that, which for me is the best job in the world! I want to help as many people as I can to make a positive difference to their personal wealth position.

My final 'why' is all about the future. Now I have two young boys and an amazing wife, and just like every other household, I want to be in a position to provide for them. But realising I am already in a very strong financial position through the investing we have already done, I now look forward to the day when I can pass on my knowledge to my two boys, so they too will have the tools to provide for their future wellbeing and families. How does the saying go? "Catch a fish and feed a man for a day; teach him how to fish and feed him for a lifetime."

Here and now

This brings me to the present where, together with Bryce and our other business partners and the rest of the great team, we help people everyday who are just the same as you to achieve their financial dreams. Helping others to grow and create wealth is a strong passion of mine that I have turned into a full-time business. I am very proud of what we have all achieved over the years.

This book is part of our ongoing efforts to help educate and impart knowledge to those who are interested in making a positive financial impact on their lives and the lives of the people closest to them, whatever their current circumstances.

Bryce Holdaway

Partner, Empower Wealth
Co-host of The Property Couch podcast
Co-host, 'Relocation Relocation Australia', Foxtel's The LifeStyle channel
Co-host, 'Location Location Location Australia', Foxtel's The LifeStyle channel
Bachelor of Commerce (Accounting, Finance & Management)
Diploma in Financial Services (Financial Planning)
Buyers' Agent
Licensed Real Estate Agent

I've always been willing to take extra risks, explore the road less travelled and stretch my comfort zone to see what's possible for me. I'm the one who is always ready to attend the latest course to give myself an edge, or align myself with a mentor to fast-track my development and help me avoid the pitfalls. I'll sacrifice my social time to listen to a keynote talk, pack up and move to another state or country, try something new, or devour the latest book on anything to do with property, personal development or better money management. I was prepared to do whatever it took to get ahead.

Looking back, I can see it stemmed from my very early fascination with the freedom that comes from having money. I desperately wanted the choices that would come from being in control of my time. Having grown up in a conservative, middle class family with two parents who had a very strong work ethic, I learned quickly that hard work was not optional – it was the only option! There was definitely no silver spoon in our household, no free rides and everything we got was a result of getting off our bums and making things happen for ourselves. However, I instinctively knew that I wanted to be in control of my own destiny and I realised very early on that it meant that I had to be in control of my finances. I knew nothing about investing or free enterprise but I can still to this day remember being about seven years old and playing with my sister and cousins out the back of my nanna's house thinking on a tangent, "I will do whatever it takes to understand the mechanics of money and how to accumulate it".

From that point on, my radar was always on and I was thirsty to learn more. In my teenage years, I was a diligent saver. I set goals for what I wanted and saved my way to get it. When I first started earning regular pay cheques, I allocated them within hours of receiving them using the old-fashioned jar system. If I allocated each portion to my yearly expenses, it ensured I never feared a bill – I had always provisioned for it and expected it. I only ever spent within my means and knew to the cent where everything went – perhaps it came as no surprise that I later studied to be an accountant. I also used to remember people simply by their car number plates. I would recall the plates before the person, so I always knew who was visiting our house or who was driving up ahead by simply recalling who belonged to which number plate. I guess I just felt comfortable around numbers. I also remember feeling that I didn't want to be one of those people who created empires out of money, or simply accumulated masses of it at the expense of others. Rather, I wanted to accumulate it to provide greater choices in my life and take as many people as I could on the ride with me; a philosophy I still hold true all these years later.

A degree of safety

My parents, older sister and I lived in a middle class suburb about 20 km south of Perth, called Bibra Lake. They bought some land in 1987, built their dream home on it and still live there today. As a pre-baby boomer born in 1939, Dad very much grew up in the shadows of the great depression and belonged in the pay-off-the-mortgage as quickly as you can camp. His goal was to provide a stable environment for his family, and he conditioned me into thinking that getting a good education was critical to me finding the right job, working for someone else and in turn providing a stable environment for my family. It would be fair to say that my risk-taking was not something that made my dad sleep well at night. My parents were initially happy when I accepted an offer to enrol at Murdoch University in 1993 and study commerce which ultimately led to me graduating as an accountant. I'm sure this made Dad sleep better as he too was an accountant and knew the job security it could provide.

While at university, instead of reading textbooks, as I should have been doing, I stumbled across the world of personal development books and tapes in the university bookshop. I was keen to learn as much as I could about human behaviour and myself in general – a passion that I still have today. That guy poring over the latest self-help book in the uni quadrangle? That was me! The guy in the library listening to the latest motivational speaker cassette on his Sony Walkman? Me again! I was an all-or-nothing kind of guy – if I found something that I was into, I would immerse myself in it boots and all. Perhaps it was at the expense of life balance, which I still wrestle with today. My wife will testify that I'm a recovering workaholic! While my uni friends were all scheming about which big six accounting firms they would try and land, I was plotting my escape from the well-worn path.

Towards the end of my degree, I jumped at an opportunity to work as a black jack dealer and poker machine attendant at the Burswood Casino, where I saw the good, the bad and the downright ugly when it came to the pursuit of money. It was a real eye-opener, and I saw some interesting stuff while I was there. After realising that there was no opportunity to quench my ambition working at the casino, to my parents' surprise, I accepted a retail position working for Cash Converters in Fremantle. The key reason I took this job was to be around my mate's dad, who had encouraged him to buy an investment property only months earlier. I thought if I worked there, I could ask him questions all day. Perhaps with hindsight, it was a touch naive and I can now see why my dad was left scratching his head.

Despite my best efforts to avoid it, the day came when I finally started working at an accountancy practice in West Perth. I was in insolvency, and I looked like a baby in a suit at the age of 22 with my overly youthful-looking fresh face. I remember my first job was to walk into a well-known franchise toy store and tell the director and business owner of some 20 years that his business was no longer in his control and if he wanted to make any business decisions he had to run them past me. This grown man broke down and wept right there in front of me and I just wanted to give him a hug! Hardly the killer instinct required for such a role.

Finding out property was my passion

The turning point in my career came in two ways back then. First, I'd seen a segment on Ray Martin's 'The Midday Show' on Jan

Somers, who came on to chat about residential property and her best-selling book, *Building Wealth Through Investment Property*. She started playing with some numbers on the whiteboard, talking about how the tenant and taxman will pay all the bills and I just remember thinking, "Oh my God. Why isn't everyone doing this?" It was a defining moment for me.

The second moment came as I just started with the accounting practice. I had heard about an investment club that held regular meetings about property investing. It was right up my alley, so I decided to drum up some confidence and attend my first meeting. I found myself in a room full of people – typically 15 to 20 years older than me – talking about property, and I was completely blown away. This was nirvana to me; like-minded people talking about property investing at a time when it was not the mainstream barbecue topic it is now. From that point on, I was like a rat up a drainpipe wanting to find out as much as I could. I went to all the meetings, got there early, stayed back late, got to know the key players and realised quickly that I was actually pretty good at talking to people despite my accounting pedigree. It was turning into a hobby and I couldn't wait for the next meeting. I was energetic, enthusiastic, ambitious and happy to do whatever it took to learn more. As a result, I became the youngest branch manager in the country at the age of 24. The guy running it eventually asked me to get involved, so I jumped in and started up a business that I ran part-time in the evenings and on weekends while I was still working full-time in my accounting job. I remember one month doing 18 workshops in 30 days all around Western Australia just to feed my need to talk about property investing. It was yet another example of jumping in boots and all.

As I began to earn more in my new part-time business, I decided to quit my full-time accounting job after 18 months, much to the amazement of my accounting colleague – and my family! By this stage, I had already learnt enough about property and I wanted to earn a living around my passion. There was just one hurdle to overcome. The founder of the club had now become my mentor, and one day he pulled me aside and said, "Sure, you're energetic, but if you want any credibility with the people you're talking to, you need to purchase an investment property". My response was, "Tell me about it! I will buy my first property as soon as it is practically possible!"

Fortunately for me, he and I joined forces. He helped me co-purchase my first property in Perth's Victoria Park in November 1999. I was 24 and we paid $199,940 for it. That led to another purchase by the two of us and then one on my own. I was driven by a strong desire to be active in the marketplace, to walk the talk myself and follow the advice Jan Somers had imparted earlier. Since then, I've owned multiple properties in multiple states across Australia, including developments, blocks of land, houses, townhouses and apartments – each with its own story and I've learned many lessons along the way.

Making my share of mistakes

One of my biggest mistakes early on was confusing activity with accomplishment. I had plenty of adrenalin in those days that fuelled my risk-taking and I loved being a part of the industry I'd yearned to work in for so long. But I learnt that just buying and transacting doesn't mean you're successful at it. For example, a failed attempt at property development on the Gold Coast in 2005, reinforced to me that long-term buy-and-hold is the way to go. I also bought the 'bling', which you'll find out more about in this book, and 'as-new', another mistake. Now I say that if you want blood-pumping adrenalin, go jump out of a plane! Successful property investing should be predictable and boring.

All of the lessons I've learnt have stayed very close to me, and I believe that they have put me in a stronger position to advise clients. I've definitely experienced the highs and lows of property investing, and I think it's important for clients to see that their adviser has been on a journey before them. I've worked from the ground up, I know what it's like and I feel I can relate to most people at every level. I think it's important to acknowledge that in the early part of my professional career, I was involved in recommending clients buy 'brand new' properties. While this is not a philosophy that I believe in any more, at the time I believed I was doing the best thing for my clients and I was buying the same properties myself. As soon as I knew there was a better way, I switched without hesitation and never looked back. I haven't recommended brand new property since 2005. Importantly though, I can still look each and every client in the eye and tell them that I did the best job I could with what I knew at the time – no smoke, no mirrors. We all get wiser with age and I won't stop in my pursuit to understand everything there is to know about property investment and become a better property adviser.

Meeting up with Ben

This leads to how I met Ben. These days I happily refer to him as my friend first and my business partner second, as well as my 'go-to' guy whenever I have a gap in my understanding of anything to do with property. I had admired Ben's passion for property from a distance for some time and I jumped at the chance to catch up for a chat when he reached out to me in 2011 to 'show me what he's been up to' with the business he founded in 2007 – Empower Wealth. I'd seen so many different people come and go in the industry up until that point and knew how to spot the wheat from the chaff. I quickly identified that Ben was different – he passionately cared about the outcomes for his clients. He was passionate too in his pursuit of the property investment truth. Importantly, he had co-engineered a 'property investment simulator' of substance that enabled him to advise his clients, based on a tailored solution rather than a cookie-cutter, off-the-shelf package. I was hooked! I remember thinking it was the missing piece and no one else could do that. It also marked the third turning point in my career as my wife and I bought into the business soon after that meeting and we have been advising clients together ever since.

Since settling down in Melbourne with my wife Andrea and our two young boys, Jack and Sam, my life has settled down too and I don't take my comfortable family life for granted. I admit I'd been something of a gypsy in the past, growing up in Perth, then moving to Brisbane in 2002, the Gold Coast, London, Melbourne and back to Brisbane, the Gold Coast and finally to Melbourne. Melbourne is my wife's home and I'm happy here. I am so very lucky that Andrea is my rock and stability. She has been by my side through all of the risks and changes, and is living proof of the importance of having the right people and the right team around you. I still devour every business and personal development book I can get my hands on, but I'm happy staying put and less likely to pack up the family on a whim to chase the next opportunity.

Location location location

Funnily enough, it was my wife who encouraged me to take a big risk in a different direction in 2010 – which led to my television career as the co-host of 'Location Location Location Australia' as well as 'Relocation Relocation Australia!' At the time, the producers at Shine Australia were hunting around for a male and female host with property experience. They got in touch with me and asked me to audition in Sydney. I kept it quiet that I lived in Melbourne. Andrea encouraged me to go for it, "so you have a story to tell the grandkids". On the plane I hopped, and somehow made it through four auditions over a period of a couple of months. I found out later that they were looking for someone to tell a story, which is exactly what I did in my auditions to camera. I never told them I was actually a natural introvert. During the auditions I turned to my old 'FORM' trick learned by another mentor – i.e. Family, Occupation, Recreation, Message – to create topics of conversation when I didn't know what else to talk about. Throw in the cameras, the lights and a few actors pretending to be clients and it's a miracle I made it!

That was five years and four seasons ago, and I couldn't have hoped for a better introduction to the world of television. My co-host Veronica Morgan and I are involved with one of the best production companies in the world – Shine Australia – screening on Foxtel's premier LifeStyle Channel. I am essentially in a privileged position to co-host my own show being a buyer's agent, pursuing my passion – residential real estate. Talk about landing on my feet. I love hitting the road and exploring all of the markets across the country. This also allows me to build greater awareness of how diverse real estate is across Australia. The shows are now screened internationally too, which is fantastic as it really brings a great profile and shines a light on Australian real estate.

To finish, I'd like to leave you with a quote from the very first cassette I listened to back in university by my favourite motivational speaker, Zig Ziglar. He said, **"You can have everything you want in life if you just help enough other people get what they want"**. I believe this to be true and I've adopted it as part of my values system ever since.

PART ONE

FOUNDATION

The state of our wallet plays with
the state of our mind

EVERY DAY, we have conversations with people about their ideas on 'wealth creation' and 'financial freedom'. It's a conversation that's hard to avoid! In the background to these conversations, is the advertising and so-called 'experts' on radio, the internet and in magazines selling the latest property get-rich-quick scheme to a bunch of unsuspecting and, we suspect, way too trusting would-be investors. The worst part about this state of play is that no-one actually knows what they have to do to achieve these ideals. If they did, surely we'd all be doing it right? Wouldn't it be wonderful for someone to wave a magic wand and reap the benefits of building wealth with zero effort? The fact that life for most of us just doesn't work that way suggests that it's possibly a little more complex than handing over some cash and receiving a glossy brochure.

That's why we are starting from the beginning. In Part One of *The Armchair Guide to Property Investing*, we explain our philosophy that **property investing is a process, not an event**. You'll hear us tap into this throughout the book, but for now it's enough to know that in order to begin your process, or journey if you like, you need a foundation upon which to build. Later on in the book, we introduce you to the nitty-gritty of investing and the tried and true strategies that we use every day. Part One is all about you and getting an understanding of where your head's at.

As our opening quote says, 'the state of our wallet plays with the state of our mind'. By this we mean that your peace of mind is directly related to the struggle that comes from having "too much month left at the end of the money" or conversely, the calm that comes from having more than enough to make ends meet. Your mindset has a massive bearing on your ability to invest successfully. Get it right and you'll be on the right track. But if you're stuck on advice from those close to you (and their personal beliefs) you should be aware that they may not understand the property market and you'll get left behind.

It's also worth mentioning that if you think you can skip this part and head straight to the strategies, you're doing yourself a disservice and you fall into the category of most Australians who cut corners and wonder why they can't get ahead. Instead, we hope you take the time to read through this section on mindset. You might be pleasantly surprised – or horrified – at what you discover about yourself!

Understanding and nutting out your own personal belief systems around property and the psychology of investing will help you in the long term by allowing you to make sound, measured and qualified decisions. After all, you're not trading marbles here, rather you're making some of the biggest financial decisions you will ever make. You need to start from the beginning because it's the only way to effectively succeed in creating long-lasting and sustainable wealth.

We can't imagine anyone on this earth not attracted to the idea of having their investments generate $2,000 a week (or more for some!) in their pocket to spend. Imagine not worrying about having to work again or being in a position to have multi overseas or domestic holidays every year, or upgrading to the latest cars or gadgets you've always wanted, or even being cashed-up enough to support your own children financially with some of their hopes and dreams.

We all want the freedom that a passive income affords us but there's a difference between the people who 'do' and those who 'wish' and that's something that we've been saying for decades: the doers know that **a financial goal without a date is just a dream.**

In Part One we also introduce you to our 'Five Essential Steps to property investing'. Irrespective of whether you're a first-timer or an experienced portfolio builder you need to read this. Like a pilot who goes through the same checklist every time he or she takes off and lands, it gives you a checklist to follow every time you invest and provides the compass to know what your next step should be at any time. It's a system and a process we developed many years ago which we personally use and our clients use every day to provide a practical way to start thinking about their own situation and what they want to achieve.

To make your learnings from this book easier to follow we'll use this pyramid to track progress and refer to along the way.

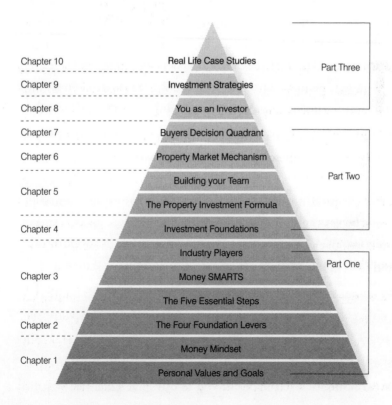

Chapter 10	Real Life Case Studies	Part Three
Chapter 9	Investment Strategies	
Chapter 8	You as an Investor	
Chapter 7	Buyers Decision Quadrant	
Chapter 6	Property Market Mechanism	Part Two
Chapter 5	Building your Team	
	The Property Investment Formula	
Chapter 4	Investment Foundations	
	Industry Players	Part One
Chapter 3	Money SMARTS	
	The Five Essential Steps	
Chapter 2	The Four Foundation Levers	
	Money Mindset	
Chapter 1	Personal Values and Goals	

BUILDING YOUR OWN KNOWLEDGE BASE

T o kick things off, we're going to talk about mindset. By this, we mean opening your mind and realising that any talk of 'money' and 'wealth' is actually a discussion about what's important to you to achieve a fulfilling life. We don't mean presenting a moral debate on how money provides happiness or how the love of money is the root of all evil, nor a hyped up 'secret powers of the mind to get-rich-quick' sermon. Instead, understanding your money and investments mindset will help give you the fuel to get cracking on your wealth creation journey, which will underline the entire process outlined in this book.

In Western society, money is seen as the number one benchmark of success. You only need to turn to the popular 'keeping up with the Jones's' saying, or watch any number of television advertisements that promote mass consumerism and aspiration to sell products. Whether right or wrong, the funny thing is that when you boil it all down, money is neither inherently *good* nor *bad*, it's just a form of barter. (We discuss this further in Part Two.)

All the same, money is somewhat of a taboo topic. We're taught not to brag about how much money we earn. This is seen as crass or vulgar. On the other hand, nobody likes to share their struggle with money socially because it's seen as a sense of failure if we can't manage it or control it. There is also the fear factor. People allow money to control them and they lack the confidence or ability to manage their money. Furthermore, people get too caught up living day to day, month to month and year to year. We reckon there are many, many Australians who live like this, too paralysed to seek out a better way to manage their finances and instead they live pay-cheque to pay-cheque.

Do you feel as if any of the following barriers to wealth ring true for you? Or are they motivators?:

→ Ill health

→ Running out of time

→ Failure to provide for your family now

→ Greed

→ Loss of a loved one

→ Acceptance

→ Envy.

As we quoted earlier, 'The state of our wallet plays with the state of our mind' and unfortunately, if you live with these fears it's more than likely your wallet will stay pretty empty.

How are our attitudes to money formed?

Our attitude to money is moulded by a number of sources, but in our experience, it's our immediate circle of influence. It's mainly through our parents, our parents' friends, our grandparents, our childhood friends and their parents, as well as our exposure to media and advertising. So it just goes to show that the apple doesn't fall too far from the tree, and it's likely the people closest to you have conditioned your attitudes.

That's all well and good if your friends and family are beautifully attuned to the ways of building wealth. But from what we've discovered it's the ill-informed opinions of others that have the biggest impact on our views, use of money and our investment results.

Unfortunately, nine out of ten Australian households think they manage their money well. They're living in a fool's paradise if they believe that because only around 5 per cent of our country's population retire financially independent. Scary, isn't it? It's our experience that the vast majority of us are unsophisticated managers of our money. We either fear money or lack the motivation to take action to build wealth.

So why don't the vast majority of people get there?

→ Lack of overall knowledge about money, investing and finance

→ Wrong mindset

→ Poor planning

→ 'Need it now' mentality – living beyond (real) means

→ Lack of understanding about value (things that grow in value and things that lose value)

→ Fear of losing money

→ Too-hard basket

→ Procrastination

→ Too time-consuming – lazy

→ Listening to the 'noise' – believing what they read and an inability to separate facts from opinion

→ Before now they didn't realise they would not have enough money for later in life

→ No discipline

→ Didn't realise how achievable it really is

→ Took advice from an unqualified source

→ No set system, strategy or structure to adopt.

Dr Kathleen Gurney, psychologist and specialist in people's money personalities, sums up our attitude to money well in her book *Your Money Personality*: *'Our feelings toward it are not static, but fluid, dynamic and sometimes intense. We love it, hate it, we fear it, we worship it, we enjoy it, but never can we ignore it.'*

Here's an interesting table that Gurney refers to on people's contrasting money attitudes. Do they speak to the way your parents or friends view money?

Figure 1: Contrasting money attitudes and conditioning

The Have-Nots and Won't-Haves	The Will-Haves
Work harder to earn more	Work less to earn more
Struggle financially	Live comfortably
Make ends meet	Feel enriched
Have a scarcity attitude	Have an abundance attitude
Find money fearful and threatening	Find money challenging and an opportunity
Believe it's their place in life	Believe anything is possibile
Place too much value on how hard it is to get money; emotional attachment controls them.	Value what money can do, seek knowledge and advice to take action and they control *it*.

Clean slate

The focus should be on what money provides us. We're all born with unlimited potential and self-esteem, so it makes sense to harness that to create a new mindset for ourselves that focuses on our end goal rather than someone else's; one that allows you to meet your personal needs and desires specifically, which is where the value is.

This is the key: attitude to money is completely individual. It's personal. It relates to what you want and your life ambitions. The greater amount of wealth you have, the better the chance of having an enriched and fulfilled life, because you have time to pursue your passions, goals and personal values.

This book focuses on creating a passive income of $2,000 per week. However in real life, we believe that true wealth is about having enough money to live completely independently in retirement and to choose to do what you want, for as long as you want, when you want. Sounds fair in love and war, doesn't it?

Personal values and money alignment

For a lot of people it's hard for them to work out what are the important things in their lives – i.e. 'the big rocks in the jar' – given all the mixed messages they get pushed on them through advertising and society in general around what success and happiness should look like. So to help you to explore what's important to you here are list of values and aspirations to think about:

→ Growth	→ Pride
→ Comfort	→ Travel
→ Security	→ Control
→ Success	→ Results
→ Optimism	→ Power
→ Stability	→ Freedom
→ Adventure	→ Better car
→ Influence	→ Fulfillment
→ Work less	→ Happiness
→ Generosity	→ Abundance
→ Relaxation	→ Self worth
→ Study again	→ Help society
→ Quiet times	→ Recognition
→ Better home	→ Compassion
→ Holiday home	→ More jewellery
→ Actualisation	→ Better health
→ Peace of mind	→ Personal time
→ Future choices	→ Accomplishment
→ Purposeful life	→ Self confidence
→ Inspiring others	→ Realising dreams
→ Time for hobbies	→ Lifestyle choices

→ Work/life balance
→ Providing for the family
→ Choose what I want to do
→ Enjoy finer things in life
→ Time with family/loved ones
→ Improved lifestyle/better standard of living

→ More big kids toys
→ Start my own business
→ Not wanting for anything
→ Volunteer/provide for others
→ Take care of myself

How many of these sound good to you? We're willing to bet a lot of them resonate with you, right? So what we want you to do is clear the slate in your head and get your mindset right by prioritising your values and aspirations and then working out how much money you will need to assist you. After all, how can you invest in property or the stock market or your superannuation if you don't know what it's all for? The greatest thing about going through this process is that it gives you a renewed sense of energy and vigour to actually implement a strategy to achieve true wealth.

The focus is to identify the values and aspirations that are important to you, remembering that they are yours and yours only – not what you think society will judge you on. These are your drivers behind your pursuit of happiness, your goal of living a fulfilling life. They are all about what you strive to attain, what you desire and they are the real motivators in your life. As we mentioned earlier, you need to understand your personal agenda in order to start your journey of money management and begin to tackle the rest of the stages in this book.

BRYCE's Mindset Messages

☐ The desire to really live a 'full' life should get you past the fear of money and investing for wealth. Most people's greatest fear is the fear of doing or being nothing. I saw two great mnemonics on Twitter recently for FEAR: 'Forget Everything And Run or Face Everything And Rise'.

☐ It's undeniable; we need money and wealth to pursue some (if not all) of our personal values and goals.

☐ The sooner you can build up sufficient wealth, you'll have more time to pursue your dreams and enjoy your financial independence.

☐ Positive money attitudes and habits can be learnt.

☐ Don't let in any further 'interference' from 'well-wishers'.

☐ Understanding who you are, what is important to you and keeping true to this will be your motivation.

☐ Your financial actions today should be driven by your willpower and desire to achieve your personal values and goals. These actions, if taken now, will provide your tomorrows with all that you desire, or the reasons and excuses why you don't.

☐ Remember, the vast majority of Australians fail to manage and invest their money successfully to achieve total financial independence.

☐ However, don't forget it's important to enjoy the journey as well as the destination!

BEN's Action Plan

☐ Sit down and document your personal values and goals. If you need an even bigger list to help you think about this, just Google 'personal values and goals' and you will find a multitude of lists and definitions to help you come up with some for yourself.

☐ Then try to put a timeframe and monetary value on your personal values and goals if you can. It doesn't matter if you record this on a scrap of paper or a spreadsheet. The key is just to get started.

☐ If achieving your goals is going to require a fair bit of cash, then have an honest conversation with yourself. If you think someone is better qualified to manage your money and invest it for you to achieve them then outsource this task. If the person you trust to do this is any good, and you don't think you are up to it, then you'll be financially far better off. (Outsourcing it now doesn't mean you'll always have to – you might gain the skills yourself one day.)

☐ You're now ready to begin learning about the Five Essential Steps to start.

THE PSYCHOLOGY OF INVESTING

2

The big take-home message from Chapter 1 is that it's possible to learn new habits to create a positive mindset. Largely, as humans, we take action based on a simple 'greed' or 'fear' basis. This means that sometimes greed can be a motivating factor for change for some people. For others it might be fear that motivates them into change. In a wealth-creation sense, the fear of not having enough money at retirement could be the spark for action. For others the desire to have riches is a greed factor. We're not too fussed about what drives you to take action to improve your financial position, whether it's fear or greed, but we certainly know that fear can starve you of opportunity because you might be fearful of failure.

The more we can break those negative mindsets and turn them into affirmative action, the more likely we'll be able to get you on the right track towards achieving your goals.

When we meet a client for the first time, and design property investment plans for them, we go through a number of processes. These are the same processes we are sharing with you in this book and the first is coming up in Chapter 3. For now, we want to give you a bit of an insight into the way *we* think a client's investment mindset plays a role. This will give you some food for thought when it comes to your own investment planning.

We call this process the 'Four Foundation Levers'. The levers are:

→ Income

→ Expenditure

→ Time

→ Target.

The key to understanding these four levers is that when it comes to any investing, not just property investing, essentially all four levers require initial attention and then ongoing monitoring. If we use the example of building a house: you'd start with the number of rooms you need (the floor plan), then its size (the measurements), then the engineering (how it's going to be built) and what it's going to be built from (building materials). Without these things you can't build the house as you planned to build it. Furthermore, if you change one of these items you automatically affect the other three. The same applies for these four levers when you are building wealth; you can't achieve this without all four and if you adjust one you impact on the others.

Naturally, within these four foundation levers there are many other things to consider and decide upon and we cover them off throughout the book, but right now from a big picture perspective, these are the true foundation levers that need our attention first. Let us explain.

Income

As is pretty obvious, what we are measuring here is income. But not just today's income – present and future income over your working life. The message here is to understand what sort of income you've got coming through now and how that's going to reduce, stop or grow over time.

Effectively you are measuring your household earnings – incoming cash on a monthly basis. As successful property investing is about managing cash flow, if you don't track income variations then you reduce your potential to build a long-term strategy, involving multiple property purchases over the journey. No smart investor should just look short term.

Things to consider:

→ What's my income going to do over time?

→ Will my career bring me incremental 'jump ups' in wages as opposed to standard inflationary increases of around 3 per cent?

→ Will my income stop at any points, for things like having a child, taking a sabbatical, and when will it resume, if at all?

→ Will my pay increase every year?

→ Can I expect regular bonuses or commission income?

→ Is my job secure?

Expenditure

Here, we're trying to understand what you spend your money on and your personal household expenses. Digging deeper, we're looking at your *essential* spending as opposed to your *lifestyle* or *discretionary* spending. There's some fantastic content on this in Chapter 3, but for now it's just enough to understand what component of your expenditure is fixed and what's discretionary 'lifestyle' spending.

It's also important for you to understand how you choose to live your life *now*. You don't want to be so focused on your retirement goal that you're living on crackers and Vegemite in the meantime, in the hope of achieving your goal way off down the track. You need sustainable solutions so you can still enjoy life along the way. Essential spending should never be cut, but in some cases there could be an agreement for reducing the level of discretionary spending if it's really high. We don't want the result to be that once you have invested in property you are breaking your back trying to make ends meet.

Things to consider:

→ What impacts on my expenditure?

→ Future expenditure plans, both one-offs and ongoing, (for example, buying a car to replace the old one is a one-off expense but starting a family soon is an ongoing expense)

→ Can I reduce my discretionary spending to focus on my bigger goals?

Time

Time is how long you've got working with income coming into your household. How much time do you have before this money that's coming in stops and hopefully the passive income that's been building up takes over? Some key questions to consider here include:

→ When am I planning to retire?

→ Is the time enough for me to do what I have planned to do?

→ Do I need to work for longer to achieve my target?

Target

What is the passive income you're trying to achieve? In this book, the target is how to generate a passive income of $2,000 per week from your property portfolio. Whether that's your exact goal or you've identified a different wealth base you want to get to, it's important to weigh up your income, expenditure and time to help you arrive at the figure you want.

→ Are my goals realistic?

→ Do I need to adjust them because they're overly optimistic?

→ Does my partner feel the same way?

In summing up, these are the four foundation levers that work in 'sync' with each other. They move and change according to what you move and change! This is really the key question – what is most important to you and what result are you looking to achieve? For example, do you want to have more income in retirement, or alternatively retire earlier, or even both? These are always the first questions to start with because, as with any goal, your target is your end destination (retirement date) when the passive income is due to kick in and you finish trading time for money. We always say that you need to start with the end goal in mind and reverse-engineer the plan. Again, a bit like building your house, start with what you want it to be and look like and then reverse-engineer it, so you have a detailed plan that is sure to work.

We realise that sounds easy but in real life when we are consulting with our clients we know some of these conversations are hard to have. We're certainly not qualified life coaches, but as trusted advisers we do find ourselves talking about serious issues within the household. For example, we ask some tough questions based on whether our clients can afford what they want and have they really thought about their ability to financially service their goals. So you need to be prepared to ask yourself the same tough questions and check to see if you and your partner both agree. In many cases there will be short-term compromises made for long-term benefit. Better you tackle these early on than wait until you're in a meeting room with an adviser you've just met!

In our experience, the biggest challenge is changing viewpoints and perspectives of our clients when they're faced with these questions. The truth is that most people are living too much for today and not living enough for tomorrow, which is where they make their first mistake. However, they've taken a great step coming to see us – just as you have by buying this book – so they're well on their way to hopefully reaching their end target.

We also have to remember that money is not the be all and end all. It's a means to an end that provides us with potential time and choices. It shouldn't be everything you focus on and money shouldn't be controlling all the decisions you make. You should identify this when you start setting your goals and priorities for your life. Money is just a commodity and we're really about trying to create more of that commodity for the household. You'll read more about this in Part Two.

These four foundation levers are the first step in making smart choices around investing in property. Once you get them right, you'll have a really good understanding of the personal mindset required to continue the next part of your plan.

Don't fall for FOMO

Speaking of mindset, ever heard of FOMO? It's an acronym for the Fear Of Missing Out. Unfortunately, property investment is rife with FOMO-ers. That is, those who are easily seduced by the headlines, get sucked in by the commentary and don't want to miss out on the 'property party' they perceive everyone else is enjoying. The reality is that you need to make sure you don't make emotional decisions on a whim and forget to 'look before you leap' to fully understand what you're getting into. Things aren't always as they seem. That means treating the 'get-rich-quick' property investment seminar with a grain of salt and avoiding the barbecue conversation where your well-meaning friend or relative tells you that place up the road is up for sale and "you should buy it as an investment!" The hope of this book is that it will stop people from investing such large sums of leveraged money as a result of FOMO!

Summary so far...

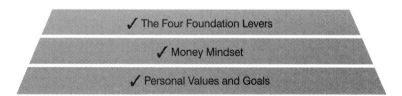

FIVE ESSENTIAL STEPS TO START

3

Sticking with our previous building analogy, if you want to build a house and think you can tackle it by yourself without any experience, you're bound to make mistakes. Sure, you can go down to the hardware store and buy the timber and bricks, measure the angle for your pitched roof and brick up around your frame. But if you are not a skilled builder and you try to do it yourself, you'll most likely have to rework it, rebuild it and there may be big time delays, which is why most people use a licensed building professional.

If you go it alone, the problems start because you should do the planning first and follow a process. Without a plan, you've got nothing to guide you, check back against (when you are not sure) or to measure your progress. We adhere to the saying from Milton H. Erikson, the American psychiatrist and medical hypnotist: *"A goal without a date is just a dream."* And here's another: *"Property investing is a process, not an event"*. We've already mentioned it, and it's a fundamental principle we live by.

Just like our two house-building examples, most people don't have a process to follow. They get caught in the microscope of property investing and don't take the time to look through the telescope for the necessary perspective. Like a yacht without a rudder, it leaves them vulnerable to whichever latest investment fad 'breeze' comes along, jeopardising them reaching their desired destination.

This chapter is about the Five Essential Steps for investors, whether you're a first-time investor or a seasoned investor with an established portfolio – it doesn't matter who you are or where you are on your property journey – everyone should follow these steps in order to achieve an optimum result.

Basically, the concept goes back to the same sort of theory around looking after our households. No two households are the same; they're all different and each one is unique. But no matter how different, or even what you are investing in, the same Five Essential Steps underpin and apply to each household. This process has been created, refined and fine-tuned to provide the essential 'tailor-made' property journey for our clients' pathways to success and now for you.

BRYCE Recommends

Ask the doctor

Have you ever felt sick and walked into a professional doctor's practice, said absolutely nothing about your symptoms, only to be quickly ushered out of the consulting room with a predetermined script and the doctor not having asked you a single question so that he can swiftly move on to the next patient? No? Of course not, because you'd be thinking, "hang on, this person knows nothing about my personal circumstances and has given me a blanket recommendation". You'd naturally feel totally ripped off!

As unimaginable as that sounds, unfortunately this happens ALL THE TIME in the property investment industry. There are one-size-fits-all strategies where, irrespective of your circumstances, a blanket recommendation is made based on the best interests of the so-called 'adviser' rather than the client. Sadly, this is not the exception but rather the norm. But it doesn't need to be… thankfully. A doctor follows the same five-step process we recommend all property investors should take.

1. **Clarify.** First, they clarify your situation by asking you leading questions about what's going on.

2. **Evaluate.** Then, they evaluate your situation, based on all the information they have gathered by talking to you and using their intuition, experience and training to reach a diagnosis about how they can help.

3. **Plan.** Next they give you a plan, e.g. a prescription or an exercise program, based on what they've clarified and evaluated. They also ensure you have understood and agree with their plan.

4. **Implement.** You walk out of the doctor's office and are advised to implement their recommendations.

5. **Manage.** Finally, you are requested to come back in a week's time. This allows the professional to manage your treatment. You tell them what you've done, based on the process and the results. It's important to note that the doctor might fine-tune the 'manage' step, and ask you to do something else, so it becomes a circular loop until you get better.

Property investment is no different. Unless it's known what's going on from the very beginning, it's impossible to go on to step two or three, because each step has to be taken in order as part of a process. Unfortunately, in the property investment space, unless there are meaningful questions asked in the best interests of the investor then you will walk out with a script – a.k.a. a property – that's likely to be a bad fit and a bad result.

The importance of this five-step process cannot be understated. We stand by it and have spent many years formulating, trying and testing it, strongly believing in the principles as a business model. We've used it and presented it to thousands of people both within and outside Australia. It's a core foundation of the advisory work we do with our clients who have gone on to invest successfully and happily build their portfolios to secure a lifetime of wealth security. The concepts are important because they work. Not only will you be able to create value in your life now but also for your future tomorrow – and who doesn't want that?

So let's get started. To give you an overview, the steps are shown in Figure 2.

Figure 2: The five step process

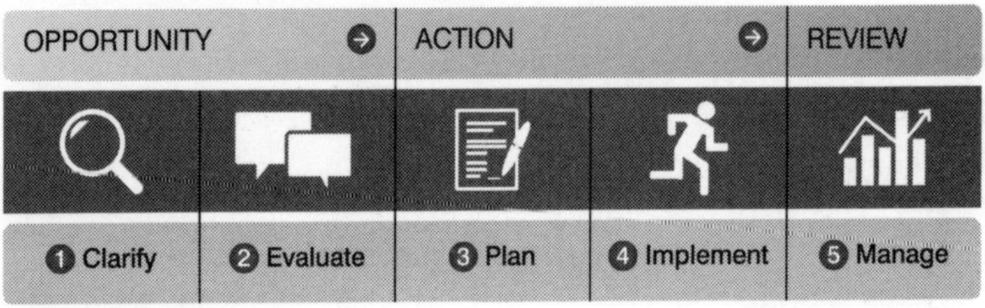

OPPORTUNITY			ACTION		REVIEW
❶ Clarify	❷ Evaluate	❸ Plan	❹ Implement	❺ Manage	

Opportunity

The first two steps are about looking at the bigger picture, creating a space in your life to take a snapshot of where you're at and where you want to be tomorrow. These steps both take into account your mindset and the four foundation levers, which we've just covered.

1. Clarify – today's preparation determines tomorrow's achievement

Let's start talking about the Five Steps. This first step is about understanding you and your household's opportunity or potential.

On a practical level, it's about collecting information about your story, both from a personal and a financial perspective. Then it's about goal-setting and looking at a short-, medium- and long-term perspective centred on what you want to achieve. This is vitally important because it will give you an understanding of what money will do for you, it will help you identify and communicate your goals and where you want to be in your life today and well into the future. Of course, your dreams and aspirations play a huge role in this first step, but it's equally important to consider the challenges, concerns and anxieties that you see that might be hindering your progress.

As we mentioned, *the state of your wallet plays with your state of mind*. So this step is about not just gaining a baseline understanding of your life, but it is also about getting down into the detail:

→ What do you spend on running your household (bills, food, etc.)?

→ What are the costs of running your car?

→ What about your phone costs?

→ How about your hobbies, such as your gym membership?

→ Where is all of your money going and what's left at the end of the day?

Unfortunately, the problem is that most people don't begin with the end in mind (you can read more about this in Stephen Covey's *7 Habits of Highly Successful People*).

To begin to clarify, you need to start with the 'destination'. You might have a dream, but you might not have defined it with a goal. So what's your dream?

→ Financial freedom?

→ More time on your hands?

→ To save for a major event, a wedding/honeymoon?

→ To be wealthy?

→ To retire at 50?

→ Be debt free?

Then what's your strategy and preferred investment vehicle to get there? That's the goal(s) and that's what you need to clarify. Once you have clarified your dreams and goals, you can move through to Step 2, evaluate, (but you should have already done this in Chapter 2)!

2. Evaluate – Success is a science

This second step is all about looking at your opportunity and potential by crunching the numbers to help you make good on your goals. But it's just as important to understand the future challenges that arise in your life, such as cash flow, which will affect your ability to achieve your goals.

So this is where we get into the numbers. Generally speaking, our process is to measure cash flow movements every month for at least 40 years. Understanding cash flow is where the real art lies in successful property investment because it usually involves debt management as well. When we can evaluate, we can really start to show how a plan can take effect.

It's this ability to measure cash flow movements that allows you to be more accurate around the value of a property and what performance you need from that property. This is opposed to a novice or an inexperienced investor who just stops at wanting the best return without understanding things like growth versus cash flow properties, global portfolios, money sitting in offset accounts or the tax impacts of every step.

For example, we see so many clients who put off investing to have a family, only to return to their investment goals in their 40s and 50s and have to scramble to catch up. With the right evaluation, they could have had a family, plus potentially secured an investment property! There are many factors to consider, but if you don't work through 'clarify' and 'evaluate' first, you won't know what needs evaluating to proceed to the next step.

In order to evaluate effectively, we need to cover off three areas:

→ **The money basics.** Putting food on the table and keeping the lights on

→ **The surplus money.** This leftover cash often goes to lifestyle but can also be put into savings or investing

→ **The bucket list.** This can be equated to the 'big rocks in the jar'. What are the must-do-before-you-die things?

How do you actually bring this all together? Luckily, through our research and experience working as advisers, we've created a step-by-step process to help you evaluate what you've got and where you sit in life financially.

We call it Money SMARTS. It's a process that we share with our clients who need an extra hand in sorting out their finances. Feedback confirms that it works a lot better than simply logging online and downloading a bank's budget spreadsheet because it takes into account much more than simply budgeting. Instead, it provides a practical way to sort out how you allocate and spend your money over the long term – not just the now. So let's interrupt the Five Steps process to look at Money SMARTS.

Money SMARTS

It's all well and good for us to advise you on what we think represents your best investment opportunities to achieve your wealth dreams, but it all really starts from superior money management. So it's time we introduced our system to help you to better manage your money. It comprises a number of key principles designed to maximise the return on your money, as well as a recommended account structure to help you take and keep control of your cash flow. We set up this system for our clients to use every day and you can get the idea if we walk you through each step.

S – Surplus

As we'll discuss later in the Money SMARTS account structure, your surplus money or cash flow is the starting point to create wealth. You simply cannot build a wealthier tomorrow or financial independence without it. It's where you capture that surplus and put it to work in either savings, paying down debt or investing it that really counts. Surpluses are established by typically working through and analysing your cash flow (income and expenditure), and it's here where you'll really start to understand your money's potential to make more money.

M – Mindset

We covered this one in our first chapter, and that's because it is absolutely critical in your path to wealth. Essentially, the trick is to adopt what we call the 'money mindset'. By this, we mean the ability to accept money simply as a commodity – an available and useful tool.

Some see money as a rare beast; scared to spend it so it sits in a bank account without earning or generating maximum wealth. At the other end of the scale are those who have no idea about what money costs, and opt for a life lived on credit, continuously buying lifestyle goods that over time lose their value or even become worthless.

Regardless of which camp you're in, the right money mindset is easy to say and harder to adopt. Everyone treats money differently and there aren't many people who actually have the right mindset. It's why we have so many clients seeking our help and why the industry is full of cowboys and sharks selling their own 'version' of wealth creation. The point is that you must conquer the first step on your road by answering this question: '*Am I going to control money or is it going to control me?*'

A – Application

This is all about you and your ability to make a real effort, by firstly taking an interest in your money, secondly making it work harder for you by establishing a plan and thirdly, being disciplined to see your plan come to life. The fact is that life throws up plenty of distractions – whether it's a business opportunity, a new temptation or personal challenge – and there's always plenty to derail us. If you can be disciplined when it comes to following the best practice principles, you'll be better placed on your road to success. **Application is all about staying the course, even when there might be the odd detour.**

R – Resources

When we talk about resources and money management, we're referring to both human and technological resources. Luckily, there are plenty of both to go around. Your human resources should be those people (your trusted network) who have done it or are teaching and advising others. When they're good, their knowledge and expertise is invaluable to help you tackle the more challenging aspects of money, such as forecasting and projection modelling. But when they're bad – be careful! We'll talk more about how to detect bad advisers later in the book.

Technology is also a fantastic resource. Technology is changing the way we track our money and more options in this space are becoming available each year. Check out some on your smart phone by searching for budgeting or money tracking.

Also, one of our favourites is the automated payment of credit cards. This enables you to take advantage of the bank lending you their money for upwards of 55 days, without ever incurring the interest charges of using the money, because the automated payment function pays off your balance, in full, each month automatically. There are also automated transfers you can set up and make to squirrel your money away to other accounts to stop you spending it. There are plenty of ways technology helps us to manage our money better, and it's great to explore these options.

T – Timelines

It's good you've done a basic budget in the past, but that's really just the beginning. What about a timeline? How else will you control, manage and plan your money around life now and into your future, taking into account your commitments and goals? A simplistic money model doesn't account for the many timeline events we need to set aside money for having kids, losing our jobs, buying a new car (although we would always strongly advise against this!), further education, a 25th wedding anniversary, or a special family holiday. These are all basic examples of looking ahead.

That's why best practice money managers are fantastic at modelling long-term timelines which take into account upwards of 40 to 50 years from now and cater for when you are going to need money and how much. But it's worth mentioning that time-lining money is an art, and although it's crucial for superior money management, it's not always easy to get right on your own. Accountants, financial planners or mortgage brokers can help you with this modelling if they are worth their salt. Just ask them if they provide these services or not.

S – Strategy

With the right strategy in place, all of the previous elements will be brought into the fold to deliver the overall money plan to be executed: from initially structuring your money and finances, then measuring surplus cash flows, to getting your mindset right and committing to the journey and the discipline required to know the resources and timelines in play. Remember the tactics will win the battle but the strategy will win the war!

The Money SMARTS account structure

Taking our Money SMARTS concept a little further, we created an account structure that enables you to think about the way you currently store, save and spend your money. As we said earlier, it's easy enough to find any number of budget tools online, but we created this one especially as a system that not only helps you identify where your money is going – which is where most online systems stop – but it's also a great way in which to establish key accounts you'll need to help you better track and evaluate where all your money goes! By following this framework, you will never unconsciously overspend again – and overspending is the hidden enemy for most households, irrespective of how much income you earn. Another great benefit of this framework is you can better funnel your money to where it matters most, because you have a good handle on your cash flows.

We know that our Money SMARTS management system works because we use it in our own lives and we advise our clients to use it as well. Now you can too and we'll show you how here.

Figure 3: The Money SMARTS account structure

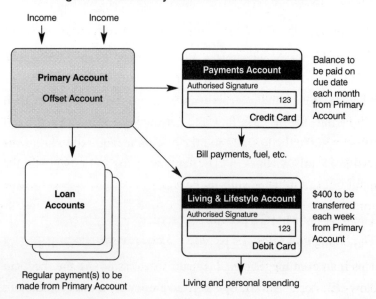

The Primary Account – The Heart

This is where the Money SMARTS system starts. Essentially, all of your income should be directed into this account and money should be taken out of this account to fund your expenses. The goal is to use it to capture your surplus income and direct it to where it will deliver the best outcome. This could be your mortgage offset, line of credit or high interest savings account depending on where you are currently sitting on your journey.

The Payments Account – Credit Card(s)

This is the danger category for a few reasons. Without the right control, it's easy to spend and end up with large debts and interest bills each month. But by setting up a credit card to pay off regular bills and vehicle expenses, you can potentially utilise the banks' interest free periods. This allows you to keep your money in the Primary Account for longer, giving you a better outcome overall.

The key is to ONLY use it for regular bills and vehicle expenses, not for unplanned or unexpected expenses, such as gifts, clothing, restaurants, luxury items. We use the Living and Lifestyle Account for these items (more on that below). You just need to make sure you pay the outstanding balance in full on or before the due date, which will avoid any interest charges. Don't draw cash out on your credit card as you'll accrue a charge, but do take out a card with the maximum number of interest-free days, taking into account the annual fee and the rewards program offered.

The Living and Lifestyle Account – The Fun Money

This is an even bigger danger category because it's where the most blow-outs occur. Any time we need discretionary money to head out for dinner, for birthday celebrations or presents, this is where it comes from. And it can easily get out of control if you're not careful!

However, we can stop this from happening because the beauty of our system lies in allowing you to set the limit of the account each month. The best way to set it up is to open a Visa or Mastercard debit card with an automated transfer from your primary account on a weekly basis. For optimum results, Thursday is the best day for this transfer to occur as you will have your money available for the weekend and if you have a 'big one' then you've got a choice to make on Monday – open up the pantry and get by with what you've got until Thursday or consciously go back to the well (the Primary Account) and top up, knowing this is eating into your future wealth. Whether your amount is $550 a week or $800 a week, that's all you'll have available to spend for that week without dipping into extra surplus reserves. If you consistently have a zero balance and find yourself reaching for the credit card, or drawing more money from the Primary Account, it's simple – you're spending more than you have planned and it will severely impact your ability to build future wealth.

Done the right way it's a powerful tool for effective cash flow management.

BEN's Tips

☐ If you wish to hold back some of the Living and Lifestyle Account money (for Christmas celebrations and presents for example), you could reduce the regular transfer by $20, which will give you $1,000 extra in the Primary Account saved up in time for Christmas.

☐ Review your credit card statement every month to check for unauthorised transactions, unexpected bill payments and more importantly, any unplanned Living and Lifestyle spending.

☐ Set up your regular payments from your Payments Account as an automatic direct debit. If your service-provider doesn't offer direct debit, try BPay and remember that these payments are perfect for things like all council rates, electricity, gas, insurance.

☐ Monitor the overall Money SMARTS system at least once a month if you are over-spending. With defined accounts it should be much easier to identify the major cash flows (incoming and outgoing) – income, loan repayments, credit card balance payments and transfers to your Living and Lifestyle Account. If you are not over-spending take a look say every three months.

☐ Remember that some months have five weeks, so there will be five weekly Living and Lifestyle Account transfers within a month. Take this into account when you're reviewing.

Action

Back now to our five-step process, the next two steps are about action. (You might want to refer back to Figure 2 on page 54.) This is where you get to put into place everything you've learned from the previous steps and really get cracking.

3. Plan – if you fail to plan, you plan to fail

If you've successfully managed to clarify and evaluate where you're at, you're ready to start planning. The reality is though that most people find it hard to put a plan into place. Whether it's to do more exercise or get a budget on the table, it's often started with the best intentions but more often than not it peters out after a few weeks. When it comes to creating a timeline for the next 40 years, this may seem even more daunting! The truth is if you don't have a documented plan, then you plan to fail. It's as simple as that.

Now, the two crucial aspects to the plan stage are strategy and tactics. Of course, we reckon one of the main reasons you picked up this book was to find out about the right strategy for you specifically, and yes, we cover this in Part Three, but it's worth mentioning here that there are many ways to create a strategy in order to help you achieve your personal and financial objectives. Our plan is to create a financial roadmap for you, and then apply the relevant tactics based on our advisory experience and expertise to provide a unique, tailored solution to property investing.

As we explained earlier, every individual is different and every household is different, so it's useless to apply the same cookie-cutter mould and expect the same result. It just won't happen. You must create your own tailor-made solution and document it.

We believe there are two metrics to help you plan your household:

→ Surplus cash flow; and

→ Measure of household liquidity.

Here we're interested in what surplus we have and our available buffer. As a general rule, we advise clients who are investing in property to have around $50,000 set aside in emergency funds. This buys you time not to panic (and should cover you for six months or even up to two years, depending on your expenses) and you'll be better prepared for any situation in the event an unexpected financial impact occurs.

 ### 4. Implement – turning best laid plans into action

This is where most people start their property investment journey in the wrong way. This is the classic case of *search rather than research,*

where they'll jump on the online portals and start checking out properties in the areas they think would make a good investment. It's something we see every day and it still amazes us that people begin here without working through the three incredibly important steps beforehand. As our doctor analogy highlighted, would you want a doctor to write you a script without a proper diagnosis? No! Yet so many people get caught by industry 'professionals' who go straight to the sell because they want your money. Or worse still, we see the DIY investor who thinks they know what they are doing and they go ahead and risk their financial future on a 'hunch' purchase.

'Implement' is where it all happens. You've got your strategy and direction – your road map – and now you're going to follow that road map because it's been properly planned to achieve the best outcome. That process is based on science which we talk about in Part Two.

You're just about to tackle the last step! Congratulations! The review and manage stage is the final hurdle, and it's just as important as the previous steps because it is all about the fine-tuning. This section ahead helps allow you to grow and control wealth for the future.

BRYCE's Tip

It's easy to understand the 'implement' step because it's the easiest to action. You may have been inspired by something in a property book, heard someone interviewed on TV about a so-called 'Hot Spot' or had a chat around the barbecue, and all of a sudden, you're in the market ready to part with your hard-earned cash. Finding any property (i.e. investment stock) is easy, but finding the right property (i.e. investment-grade) is where employing an experienced and qualified buyer's agents will pay dividends with your asset selection. They will have a clear objective that is measurable against performance criteria, rather than the 'I reckon I'll just have a go' mentality. Just a 1 per cent better performance over 10 years can have a huge impact on the value of your portfolio and ultimately the amount of passive income you will have when you retire. A buyer's agent fee should be reviewed in the context of the net result to your portfolio rather than simply just seen as a cost centre in isolation.

Review

5. Manage – what gets managed gets done

Manage is all about 'measure and monitor' and checking in; it allows you to take a step back and have a good look at what's been achieved and benchmark those results against your plan. Surprisingly, this action often gets left out and becomes the forgotten step. When it comes to monitoring, it's just like our doctor's analogy, where you might head back to the practice to get checked up at various points over the following months.

It's worth noting that the property investment industry as a whole performs this function particularly poorly. A good property investment adviser will arrange to see you for a check up annually, while the bad ones don't even give you a plan and never follow you up once they have made their sale and their commission on you. Sadly, there are plenty who fall into the latter category!

Review your plan and stick to it

I've got a story I love to tell that perfectly highlights the importance of the manage stage. I had a client who came to me in 2010, who was an international flight attendant. Her life was spending every second weekend in London and every other weekend in Sydney. She explained that her well-intentioned plan was to buy an investment property each and every year after she purchased her first one in 2002. This way she would take advantage of the surplus cash she was accumulating at the time. So given I met her eight years on from this initial purchase you'd suspect she'd have up to eight properties if she'd kept her pledge. Naturally I asked her, "How many do you have now?". To which she replied, "I've still only got the first one and I haven't purchased since!" Her response to my quizzing her about why was simply, "Sadly, I just haven't got around to it." It's the classic case of life getting in the way and opportunity being missed. If you don't make a plan and review it every year, that's exactly what happens... LIFE!!

Property investment is not something where you can just buy the paper every weekend and check out whether your stock levels have gone up and down, which plays with your mindset. Instead, great property investment should only take about 10 hours per property a year to manage – from your armchair! That's nothing! You can just peek over the fence (figuratively of course), check in with the property manager about how everything's going, find out when the next review is, check that the tenant is happy and then get on with living your life. We'd suggest having a bi-annual property review, and then your responsibility is to manage your cash flow so you can execute your second and subsequent purchases as your plan requires.

Free or fee advice?

Now that you know the Five Essential Steps, it's a good idea to have a solid understanding of how the industry works. You've probably been in situations where you've been cornered by someone chatting to you and trying to sell you a 'never to be repeated opportunity' in the form of a development or property and you've been unsure of their possible hidden agenda.

Now, this section might not make us popular in our own industry but in the interests of transparency and giving you the right tools you'll need to make investment decisions, we think it's important to share this information with you. We'll look at the ins and outs of the industry, who are the major players when it comes to the investment property process, and how they all get paid. Understanding this will be a huge help to you when you cross paths with any of these operators but they can be guarded, so you need to know what to look out for.

Essentially, you have two options when it comes to receiving a service from someone in the property investment industry. You will have a choice between a **free service**, where the professional receives a sales commission by acting in the seller's best interests, or a **fee-paying service** where you pay a fee directly to an adviser who is acting in the best interests of the buyer. The key is to ask yourself: "Am I being offered a choice?", "Is the advice independent?", and "What is the best property for me?" If the adviser wants to know more about your specific circumstances before they make a recommendation, that's a great sign. If they immediately point you towards a particular property – a warning alarm should sound. Returning to our doctor's analogy, you wouldn't write a script without understanding the patient, and it's the same with property.

Another way to look at it is to break it down to these two questions:

→ Are they selling me something?; or

→ Are they advising me?

So next time you head off to see your property investment adviser, just have these questions in the back of your mind. Are they giving you advice or are they just facilitating a transaction? The advisers who understand investment, strategy and structure are the ones to seek out and keep a hold of!

Meet the industry players

Now it's time to introduce you to the major players and explain who is offering a fee for service or a free service. Here are the blunt facts – most of these guys don't really want you to know how this all works. That's because unlike other professions, such as solicitors or doctors, there is NO education or qualification entry level to become an adviser on property. Yes, it is shocking and as a result, this makes it all pretty easy for the spruiker to throw on a nice suit, get a hair cut and begin booking out their seminar sessions because that's pretty much all they need to get started! Talk about minimum barriers to entry with significant income on offer to those with a silver tongue! It seems crazy to us that so many people are ready to part with large sums of money on the advice of someone who is ill-equipped and unqualified to give it. Therefore, it's invaluable to get underneath the shiny suits and really understand how everyone works in the industry.

Figure 4: The industry players

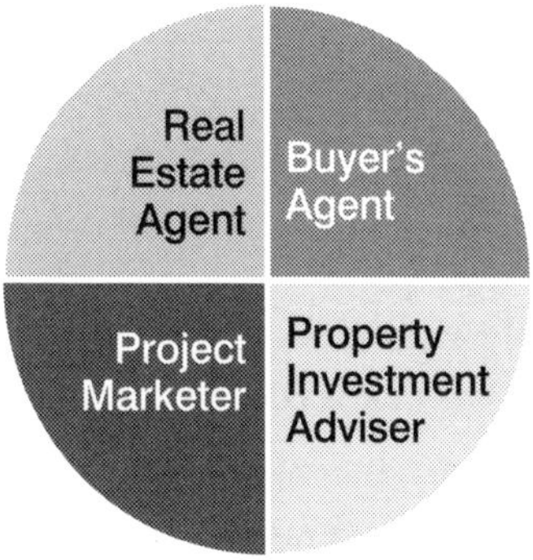

This framework gives you a thorough breakdown of who's who in the zoo. Let's start with the left-hand side of the quadrant – the real estate agent and the project marketer. These guys operate in the free-advice component of the industry. You're more than likely to come across these guys. They'll give you free information in the form of brochures or flyers, and also enable you to buy property that they're offering for free (i.e. you pay the property's price with no additional payment to the agent). This is because their client is the seller of the property. Let's break it down:

Real estate agents:

→ Mostly sell established properties

→ Their client is the seller; not the buyer

→ Earn their income by selling and receiving a portion of the purchase price; if they don't sell they don't eat

→ Typically earn anywhere from 1 to 3 per cent of the purchase price (usually it's 2.5 per cent).

Project marketers:

→ Only sell brand new properties, e.g. an-off-the-plan, high-rise apartment buildings or house-and-land package deals, or townhouse developments, etc.

→ Get paid by the developer to sell their stock

→ Typically earn anywhere from 5 to 10 per cent of the purchase price.

(Warning: Some of these operators will call themselves Property Investment Advisers – so it's always best to ask how are they paid.)

On the right-hand side of the quadrant, we move into the **fee-paying** scenarios, of which there are two: the buyer's agent and the property investment adviser. These guys are fee-for-service providers, which means their income is derived from the money they charge their clients. Let's break it down again:

Buyer's agents:

→ Work for the buyer to find the best property in the marketplace that's in the buyer's best interests

→ Charge a fee to act for their client

→ Work on the 'Implement' part of the Five Essential Steps to Start formula

→ Charge a professional fee, typically represented by either a percentage of purchase price or a flat fee (which we think is preferable)

→ Must hold a valid real estate agent's licence.

Property investment advisers:

→ Perform each of the Five Essential Steps to offer an end-to-end professional service

→ Work for the buyer

→ Charge fixed planning fees, usually from $2,000 for a single property recommendation up to $4,400 for a full multiple-property investment plan. (Pricing is very similar to what fee-for-service financial planners charge.)

→ Might offer an annual ongoing review fee of $500 to $1,000 per year to help manage and review a client's property portfolio.

So next time you're at a property expo or seminar event where you're being flooded with information, stand back and ask yourself how are these guys getting paid and where do they fit into the quadrant. Are they more interested in the glossy brochures on their trestle table, or are they focused on your situation personally? Are they forthcoming about how they are getting paid if you ask them, or are they cagey? It's OK if it's the latter as long as you exercise caution and don't do anything crazy like hand over your holding deposit without finding out more first.

As property advisers ourselves, and as we've explained at length so far about building the foundation, successful property investing is not a one-size-fits-all scenario. Every single person and story is different and this requires different solutions that are tailor-made to suit their circumstances.

BRYCE's Tip

Successful investors are successful because they are educated – it's as simple as that. The good ones understand how the industry works and know what to do to achieve their goals. So here's a tip: if you don't know what an LVR is (for the record, it's Loan To Value Ratio), you might want to reconsider making a big property decision. Or at least you should make the decision when you have a better idea of what's involved in investing, how the market works and who the players are in the industry.

Property investing is not a short-term investment. It's not enough to just find a property, sign on the dotted line and expect the cash to flow into your account the next day. The whole process starts with you getting your mindset right, understanding where you sit financially, finding the right property in the right market, negotiating a good price, finding a qualified and experienced property manager, to name just a few things you need to consider. Success does not come without the sacrifice of educating yourself properly or engaging experienced advisers to help you. Remember this: property investing is a game of finance, whereas buying your own home is a game of bricks and mortar. Just because you live in a property doesn't mean you know how to invest in one!

PART ONE WRAP-UP

To wrap up Part One, the biggest message we want to leave you with is that **building a property portfolio is a process, not an event.** If you think you're set for life after transacting a property after just one weekend, you're mad. As we've just explained, there are five critical steps to work through if you're serious about building a portfolio:

1. **Clarify** your position and identify your short-, medium- and long-term goals;

2. **Evaluate** the sort of tactics you need to adopt that suit your investor profile as it relates to debt and retirement;

3. **Establish** a plan that models your cash flow in the future as well as for today;

4. **Implement** the plan with an understanding of what makes an investment-grade property in an investment-grade suburb;

5. **Manage** your portfolio's ongoing performance, monitor and fine-tune your plan over time.

Unfortunately, many investors dive straight into the implementation phase and end up losing out in the long term. They don't realise how important it is to work on the first phases in the beginning. They buy something inappropriate and it's all a bit too little too late. It's also helpful to understand the key players in the industry – did you recognise any of these?

There is so much more to property investing than simply searching online in your lunch break, which brings us neatly to Part Two. Here, we dive deeper into the theory of property. It's all well and good to have the right mindset but if you don't actually understand the theory and the science of the property market, you'll unfortunately be flying blind.

As you continue reading you might be surprised at just how complex investing in property can be. It's certainly much more difficult to master than the real estate agents and property marketers make it out to be. But with a more thorough understanding of the technical side of the market that you'll get from the next section, and by giving you the right signs to look out for, you'll be well on your way to property investing success.

Summary so far…

✓ Industry Players
✓ Money SMARTS
✓ The Five Essential Steps
✓ The Four Foundation Levers
✓ Money Mindset
✓ Personal Values and Goals

PART TWO

THEORY

"An investment in knowledge always
pays the best interest."
—BEN FRANKLIN

THE ARMCHAIR GUIDE TO PROPERTY INVESTING

IF PART ONE is all about setting out the principles and foundations, then Part Two takes you to the next level by focusing on the 'nitty gritty' of property investing. We've given you our successful steps to start the process, which we believe is the only way to effectively begin to take on and manage a property portfolio. Now it's time to delve into the industry as a whole to give you a sound understanding of how it works, as well as introduce you to our property investment formula.

You may not have realised it yet but you've already learnt so much about what makes for a good property investment. Have you noticed a trend? So far, it's been all about *you*. We've discussed learning about *your* mindset, *your* essential steps to start, *your* understanding of the industry and *your* roadmap to success.

What about the property market itself? While it's critical to get your mindset right, have your foundation set and your Five Essential Steps all planned out in advance it doesn't really help you know and understand where to actually invest your money. We've been in this industry for decades and have a pretty good appreciation of the machinations of the property investment game, but if you're a novice or think you're an expert because you've secured your one property in the last ten years then think again. You'll want to read on to see how we unpack the market. You'll find out how we see the property market really work behind the scenes and how to make it work for you so that it caters for your individual circumstances.

In this part of the book, we'll show you the fundamentals to investing so you can see an overall view of the industry, as well as the A, B, C and D that makes up our property investment formula. Master this and you'll be well placed to climb the investment ladder with confidence and surety.

We also share our insights with you on what we call the 'science' of investing, taking you through concepts such as big data, lead and lag indicators and their relationship with supply and demand. You need to know how to develop an analytic eye when it comes to identifying investment-grade property – without it you're more likely to run into trouble. That flashy apartment looking so good in the glossy brochure may not be as good an investment as you think it will be. We'll show you what to look for to avoid the pitfalls.

It's why we call it the 'nitty gritty'. To be a successful investor, you need a solid understanding of how property works: where to invest, the psychology of pricing and property analysis. Don't worry, we won't be too scientific and technical but our purpose here is to show you that a deeper 'human' understanding of the property investing process is just as important as learning about you and your goals.

Just as the science stuff is great to know, it's also valuable to understand and be aware of the human drivers behind property. That's why we've included our buyer's decision quadrant in Part Two which really gets into the heads of the how, what, where and why people buy what they buy. Our philosophy is that mindset and human indicators are intrinsically linked to property. If you can ride on the coat-tails of this when you're investing, you're half way there.

THE FUNDAMENTALS OF INVESTING

The reality is that the earlier you start investing, the better off you'll be. But there's no denying that life gets in the way, and all too often we see clients walk in the door quite late in their potential wealth-building journey. While we never doubt our ability to achieve great results for them, it might involve more work and risk than if they'd started the ball rolling years earlier. For that reason, both time and timing are fundamental to building wealth.

Risk is another fundamental factor. Everything involves risk and when it comes to money management and investing, the stakes can be (and are) high. We always advise clients to consider all of the risks for every possible investment outcome, because it's vital to be comfortable with whatever level of risk you are willing to take on.

If we're talking risk, it's also important to mention personal risk. You are the most valuable asset in your life, so you need to ensure you are protected as best you can be. You need to take adequate insurance against any adverse life events that will materially affect your portfolio building, such as sickness and/or temporary loss of income. This cost should be included in your Money SMARTS calculations, which we covered in Chapter 2.

So why invest in property? What are the risks versus rewards when investing? Once you've secured your investment, how do you manage it? These are all important questions to ask yourself if you're contemplating going down the path of investment. After all, you've laid the right foundations. You've got an understanding of your mindset and you've learnt about the Five Essential Steps, so now it's time to get to grips with the nitty gritty. But first, you need one final lesson to best understand money, from an investor's view point.

 BEN Asks: Did You Know?

☐ Better personal health and medical technology will increase life expectancy. In 2050, the average male will live to 92.2 years old and the average female will live to 95 years. Living longer will mean we need a greater wealth base to sustain our retirement.

☐ More than 62 per cent of couples retire on less than $20,000 per year.

☐ Only 10 per cent of the current retired population have an income greater than $43,000.

☐ You need $1,000,000 in net income-producing assets outside of your family home, returning 5 per cent p.a. to generate a passive income of $50,000 per year, on-going. Therefore, you need $2,000,000 to generate an income of $100,000 without touching the capital base. And that's in today's terms – not accounting for inflation!!!

What is money?

OK, so let's talk money. Now, just bear with us (or perhaps humour us) for a few moments as many of us missed getting the basics about money taught to us in school. So, what is it? Technically, money is a form of barter used for the purchase of goods and services. It makes the world go round and the more money we have access to the more goods and services we can exchange. Day to day, we need money for everyday survival. It provides the modern means to clothe us, feed us and to secure both our 'needs' and our 'wants'. Over time, money has become the preferred form of bartering, surpassing the likes of gold and other precious metals and from the very early times of working for the return of food and water.

At one extreme, the lack of money can restrict us from receiving basic and essential needs, such as shelter, food, clothing and water to other opportunities such as living standards and lifestyle desires. At the other extreme, money is extremely powerful. It's a catalyst for progress and as the preferred form of barter it has allowed us to more widely and freely choose and exchange it. This has led to the development of an overall marketplace, where goods and services are supplied in exchange for money, with that money moving through overall economies. These marketplaces comprise buyers and sellers driven by supply and demand.

When you combine the mini sub-marketplaces in a country, they form the overall market place of a country or population – its economy. When different countries deal with each other they use a money exchange known as the foreign exchange marketplace. This is where the value of one country's currency is valued against that of another, using the market forces of supply and demand.

In fact, money is the biggest commodity on the planet, far surpassing any other commodity in value such as gold or oil, because in simple terms gaining access to money is not only critical to our individual survival, as we discussed, it's also critical to the survival of countries themselves. It is fundamental to a global economy; without it, the world's economies stop. This is best illustrated with the recent GFC (Global Financial Crisis) in 2007-08 or as we saw it, 'Global Freeze on Money' as nations and businesses stopped lending to each other at that time.

What is wealth?

Wealth is measured by the combination in value of:

→ The 'appreciating' assets you hold less the borrowings held against them. This includes property and direct shareholdings (when they are increasing in value and/or the companies are paying dividends). The other item to include as an appreciating asset that many of us don't recognise, but which is technically critical to the whole picture, is YOU and your ability to 'source' money, usually via earning an income or profits from the work you perform, but it does come usually from other sources.

→ The amount of savings and investments you have. This includes bank deposits earning interest, term deposits, bonds, superannuation and managed funds.

While wealth is pretty easy to measure and understand, the majority of people make mistakes when they measure their wealth because they include assets that historically depreciate, such as new cars, home contents, motorbikes, boats, caravans, music or DVD collections, televisions, computer and electrical equipment. All of these items depreciate in value over time and add no material value to your net worth over the long term.

How do you create wealth?

Creating wealth has several components and variables, but essentially it's created by:

→ **Accumulation.** This is your ability to acquire more assets, income and savings, which builds greater wealth for you over time

→ **Growth/return.** The measure of the increase (or decrease) in value of your assets over a period of time

→ **Protection.** This is all about the ability to protect the value of the assets. In good times this should result in the value of the asset growing and in the tough times it should limit the downside risk of the asset losing value

→ **Time, risk and skill.**

On its own, wealth may be seen as a measure of possessions (assets) and money at a moment in time, but together, wealth creation is the trial and error of managing all of the components and variables to find your 'safest and most reliable' pathway to your end financial goal.

Now you've had your 'fast track' history lesson on the basics of money and wealth creation, let's discuss the best ways to get hold of it.

Generating money

There are four ways we access or generate money.

Work

This is the most obvious way to obtain money. You can work as a PAYG employee to earn income or you can be self-employed and earn money through income or profits from your own business. We give up about a third of our time working on the tools to earn money, and for most of us, it's our primary money generator.

Charity/government support

These are charitable donations or government pensions. Charity money is a hand out usually offered to the needy but it could also come from a wealthy individual or entity providing to others, such as a wealthy parent gifting funds to their son or daughter or grand-kids. However, it's often an unreliable – or inconsistent – source of money or income.

When it comes to government pensions, our elderly citizens could correctly argue they deserve ongoing monetary assistance for later on in life because they worked and paid their taxes and no super-annuation scheme existed way back then. Yet the risk is that the government of the day might not have enough funds to go around which could mean the pension income is low and remains low. People looking to retire should never rely on it! This book is all about becoming a self-funded retiree, where you take control of your destiny and you get to choose how much you are going to live on.

Investment returns

This is monetary return from income or increases in capital value. Examples of this include the interest earned on savings with your bank, dividends from shares held, rental income and increases in the capital value of your investments. The great thing about investment returns is they use your money to generate more money over time, and in the majority of cases the money generated is through passive activities that don't involve a lot of your time. They simply build up over time, but only if they're stable and sound investments. This is where we start to talk about the 'A' of asset selection in our property investment formula.

Borrowings

This is the 'B' in our property investment formula (more in the next chapter) and it's about accessing money via borrowings to build greater wealth. Fundamentally, most businesses operate by borrowing money every day to fund and expand their operation. And you, as an individual, are pretty much the same. You should be calculating the potential return of your selected investment against the risks that that investment asset may carry, keeping in mind that the bigger the borrowings, the bigger the risk.

So to sum up, borrowing money is a way of accessing other people's money – usually a lender's – to gain an improved outcome. The lenders are usually happy about lending it because they are also keen to generate money, which they do by lending their own money at a higher rate than they paid to source it. This is why the money you have in the bank traditionally earns less interest than the interest you pay when borrowing the money from a bank.

BEN's Business Borrowing Examples

An example is a wedding car hire business which needs to borrow money to purchase two more cars because demand for their services is so strong. They consider the costs of borrowing the money versus the forecast income the new cars will generate to see if there is money (profit) in their hand after all costs are covered. On a larger scale, a department store seeking to expand contemplates installing another floor for more retail space to sell their goods. They too forecast the planned expenditure over the life, time and cost of this against the income they believe they can generate. Once again, if they believe they can generate more money than they pay out, as well as weigh up the risk of borrowing the money, keeping in mind what might go wrong, they would probably go ahead and borrow the money.

 BRYCE's Money Tip

Don't ever borrow money for non-appreciating assets or investments, such as holidays, household goods and cars! This is a sure-fire way of limiting your wealth-building potential and you will more than likely be another statistic who's living off charity and the government for the rest of your days in retirement. In the car example, if you absolutely NEED a car because without it you can't get to work to start generating income from which to build wealth, look for a second-hand car that is reliable and safe enough for you to get to and from work – and one that's economical to run too!

Influencing the value of money

It's all well and good to generate money. After all, you need to earn money to make more money. But you also need to understand how to influence money, and in doing so, establish whether money is controlling you or you are controlling it.

Money costs or controls us in different ways. Do these ring a bell: living costs; interest on personal debt, credit card interest, car loans, lifestyle debts; inflation; tax? These are all costs and in a way they control us because we have to pay them back.

Inflation for example, plays a big part in the value of money, but because money loses value over time due to inflation, it's not often understood by most and can be the hidden cause for people not achieving their wealth goals. Basically, inflation is defined as a general rise in the level of prices of goods and services. It's measured by the CPI (Consumer Price Index) which moves over a period of time to indicate the percentage rate of inflation present within the economy or marketplace. Here's a simple example: if you had $100,000 today, it would be worth less – $85,873 – in five years' time if you kept it under your mattress, if inflation is growing at 3 per cent. Not really a sound wealth-building strategy, is it?

On the other hand, if you had $100,000 invested in an asset that had a hedge against inflation and which was growing at 3 per cent, your $100,000 would be worth $115,927 in five years' time. This is because inflation has the ability to accelerate the value of appreciating assets, such as houses.

So depending on your approach to money, it can cost you or you can control it to make more of it. If you have an investment approach to money, it can make even more money when it's invested to achieve capital growth as well as income (yield) returns. We talk more about this in Part Three, but right now, it's enough to know that:

1. Capital growth is basically when the demand for the asset pushes its value higher; and

2. Income or yield is when the asset produces an income which could be in the form of rent, dividends or interest earned from an investment.

BEN's Tip

Capital and yield returns are not mutually exclusive. You can get both, but usually the higher the capital return the lower the income return and vice versa.

So now let's introduce two of the best ways we use money as a means to accelerate the wealth outcome of an investment. These are leverage and compound growth.

Leverage

Leverage is the controlled use of borrowed money to purchase part or all of an asset in the hope that it'll make a profit that's more than the interest payable on the borrowings. Just as in Ben's business borrowing examples earlier.

In property, you might use a relatively small amount of money to make a purchase, with the majority provided by a lender. Let's take a very simplistic example, excluding all costs. Let's say you pay 20 per cent of a $500,000 investment property, so your initial investment is $100,000. Over 12 months, that property appreciates at 5 per cent giving you an asset value of $525,000. If you'd used the same $100,000 to buy a property outright costing $100,000 and assuming the same 5 per cent of appreciation, your asset value would have increased only $5,000, instead of $25,000 for the more expensive property (see Figure 5). That difference of $20,000 represents the use of leverage. Naturally, if you measure these returns over a 20-year time span, the impact of leverage is even greater and so are the investment returns.

The key to leverage/borrowing, is selecting the right asset or investment, because the success of this strategy relies on appreciation. This is covered off in the next chapter with our tried and tested property formula, so keep reading.

Leverage also carries a high risk. The property might not appreciate or it might even fall in value, or the cost of borrowing the money might exceed your ability to repay the loan, requiring you to sell it, which could mean a big loss.

Put simply, leverage is a means to magnify the investments you hold, just like the wedding car business now operating more cars to make a greater return. In property investing, it's all about controlling a higher value of property to increase your returns. (But if you get too greedy and over-extend yourself, it can turn very nasty very quickly, which is why we have spent so much time talking about cash flow and money management.)

Figure 5: The power of leverage

Example	Investment #1	Investment #2
Cash to invest (equity or savings)	$100,000	$100,000
Compounding returns	10%	10%
Can afford to buy	$100,000	$500,000
Debt	$0	$400,000
Loan to value ratio (LVR)	0%	80%
Return on investment (ROI)	$10,000	$50,000
Interest costs (6%)	$0	$24,000
Net return ($)	$10,000	$26,000
Cash return	10%	26%

Compounding

The legendary scientist Albert Einstein said compounding was "the most powerful force in the universe", and he also deemed it "the eighth wonder of the world". We tend to agree. Compounding is essentially the ability of an asset to generate its own earnings, which are then reinvested to generate their own earnings. It can have an excellent impact on your financial position because the growth earned over a period of time is added to the collective principal amount. A great way to see the impact of compounding growth is in this graph:

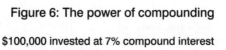

Figure 6: The power of compounding

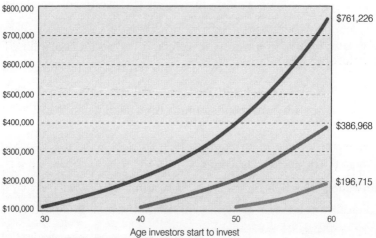

$100,000 invested at 7% compound interest

We can see here that the age at which you start to compound your returns has a clear impact on your financial position, and it's a measure and forecasting tool we use every day for our clients.

Investing

So now that we know a little more about money and wealth-building, let's bring the conversation around to investing which is why we're all here. First, why do you need to invest? Perhaps some of your values are listed here:

Greater wealth to provide a better quality of life during the middle and retirement years

We are blessed in this country to have one of the highest standards of living in the world. When you are young and earning money, it's great to be able to buy new things, treat yourself to fabulous holidays or a night (…or three) on the town. All of this smelling-the-roses stuff is great, and with modern households usually having both adults earning an income, why not enjoy it, right?

Well, that's fine as long as you put aside some money for tomorrow because it'll be a huge shock to the system when one day you finally get around to thinking about retirement only to realise you have only enough wealth to generate a yearly household income of, say, $30,000. The problem here is that you will have become very accustomed to your current lifestyle and living standards that cost more like three times this amount! In this example, given you have insufficient appreciating assets and savings, your $30,000 a year is typically broken down into 75 per cent of income generated from the return of the assets, and the remaining 25 per cent is actually made up of selling down your assets. This means you'll soon run out of your own wealth and have to live off the measly government pension for the rest of your life. It's not that appealing is it? Unfortunately, we can't recall time and start over so it's scary stuff indeed when you're confronted with the reality of how your retirement might actually look.

Instead, your aim should be to factor in the lifestyle and living standards you want to enjoy in retirement and work out what they would cost. Take out whatever costs you currently bear – for example, your kids' commitments, mortgage and other loan repayments – because you certainly don't want to carry over significant debts into retirement which will be an added burden in the earlier or active years of retirement.

To help you, it can be worthwhile jumping on to some of the banks' websites to use their online tools that calculate the level of income you are going to require. The bottom line is if you're able to start your wealth creation journey early enough, then there is no reason at all why you shouldn't be able to achieve your retirement goals.

Less reliance on government handouts, such as the pension

Superannuation is simply a forced savings scheme introduced to reduce the burden on government to fund retirement pensions. The federal government introduced compulsory superannuation in 1993, after treasury provided the government of the day with forecast analysis relating to the pending retirement of the baby boomers and the imposing costs government would have to fund once this generation retired. We can see this starting to play out for the current government, in terms of the pressure and cost of funding pensions for those who weren't able to fund their own retirement.

The government has several strategies available to help it cover its pension liability. It can:

→ Adjust the retirement age (i.e. increase the access age to the pension)

→ Adjust the income and assets thresholds

→ Adjust the amount of pension they pay to singles and couples

→ Restrict the amount of additional income you can pay into your super fund (without getting taxed at a higher rate of tax)

→ Through a 'transition to retirement' phase, restrict how much you can withdraw from your super fund

→ Increase the percentage employers have to pay as compulsory superannuation contributions

→ Increase taxes on employee contributions

→ Introduce a tax on earnings and income post retirement.

We often hear or read about the push to increase compulsory super contributions up to as much as 15 per cent because retirees are chronically 'under saved' to support themselves in retirement. When we look at all the options the government has at its disposal, we personally believe that super isn't the silver bullet solution – not for us, our families, or our clients for that matter. That's why we are taking control of our financial futures.

Opportunity for 'future choice' and/or to retire earlier

When we think about total financial independence, we mean the ability to substitute work time for other activities, pursuits or interests, at that time when we already have enough wealth built up from other sources. For us, that money is in the form of our investments in residential property, which produce passive income in the form of rent. Having ongoing access to this passively generated money provides us with the time to allocate to these other areas in our lives. This means that we may be able to retire when we choose to because we have sufficient income to provide for our independence. The choices we make from this point forward could include working less, not working at all, doing some community or volunteer work, travelling more, or basically whatever our hearts desire and wallets can cater for.

However, everyone's target of financial independence is different. We talked earlier about the level of lifestyle to which we get accustomed: some of us don't want to give away these creature comforts, while others want to continue to build wealth, even during semi or full-retirement by moving money around to obtain better investment returns. Furthermore, some of us are content in the knowledge we have built enough wealth to provide for our expected retirement years, and draw comfort from the knowledge that once we retire we won't ever have to go back to work.

Ability to provide a better standard of living for your family, as well as for future generations

Many people are motivated to provide a better standard of living for their family. This is almost a built-in desire in us all. In our experience, providing a suitable home or accommodation for our family is one of the most commonly mentioned desires of our clients. The other popular motivations are health for everyone in the family – from the kids to the grandparents – as well as to provide the best level of education that can be afforded for children, or planned future family. Family time often then follows, usually in the form of holiday time. These core desires all provide a better standard of living and once again wealth creation should provide greater access to money and time.

An important footnote to this is that you need to be very clear about the costs of your standard of living. If you get this out of balance, you could end up working another 20 years longer than you had hoped, because you mismanaged the allocation of your money and or invested poorly.

Philanthropy

The ability to be a dedicated philanthropist is a wonderful achievement. We think everyone should consider giving back to the community in some way if they are more fortunate than others and that a contribution to the greater good should be everyone's goal. Philanthropy comes in many forms: providing donations, materials, assets and of course your time.

Provide for future generations

This is very similar to the 'better living standards' point above, however true wealth can provide for not just your family now, but also many future generations. It can provide your family with a wealth base to grow generational or 'legacy' wealth as we call it. You could maybe even strive for a dynasty! We often hear and read of grandparents wanting to pay for their grandchildren's education, and you can bet financial planners are very happy to oblige in setting up education investment funds from either grandparents or parents.

Access to better health care services in the future

Our final 'why invest' point is about health. We have touched on the ability to provide suitable health care for our families but as most of our clients are in their mid-20s to mid-40s, they're more concerned about being in a position to protect their children's and ageing parents' health, especially if they don't have the income or savings to access superior health cover. If your family is currently facing some concerning health matters, you'll know exactly how close to home this hits and how important it is to have the ability to fund the required health insurances and medical costs that give your family immediate access to superior care and specialist treatment.

Investment choices

Next up, let's consider the types of available investments. Essentially, these include:

→ Fixed interest/bonds

→ Cash (e.g. bank interest through high interest bank accounts, term deposits, cash management accounts)

→ Direct property (our recommended favourite as it relates to residential and commercial)

→ Shares – Australian and international

→ Alternatives – Real Estate Investment Trusts, agribusiness, wine, art, antiques, collectables, coins, etc.

It's possible to own investments via a number of different ownership structures, each offering various tax benefits or asset protection. These include owning an investment in your own name, through joint names (individuals), in a company name, a trust's name or a superannuation fund's (SMSF's) name.

Typically, you'll have a team of investment professionals to support you along the way, which might include:

→ **An accountant** – with experience in trusts, companies and self managed superannuation funds (SMSFs), tax minimisation and money management

→ **A solicitor** – to assist with asset protection, wills, property transfers and guarantees

→ **A financial planner** – to advise on superannuation, SMSFs, managed funds, shares and regulated investments, personal insurances and pension planning

→ **A finance adviser/mortgage broker** – for your credit planning, loan sourcing and structuring and money management

→ **A property investment adviser** – to assist with your property investment strategies, recommendations and planning

→ **A buyer's agent** – who will be responsible for selecting, negotiating and securing investment-grade property assets.

All of these professionals will be equipped to help you get the ball rolling, but you'll also need to think about where you sit as a long-term investor. In our experience, the mindset of the long-term investor is often based on fear or greed and both present a high risk to wealth creation. Why? Because fear leads to inaction or pro-crastination and you don't do anything; and being too greedy could result in you getting in over your head, which can be dangerous. We talk more about how to engage the right adviser in the next section.

Just as we started this chapter, let's once again remind you that it's crucial when dealing with money to not only understand how money works but also to have a thorough understanding of the risks involved. It's the only way you can proceed with a level of confidence. Here's another graph that profiles the risk versus return by investment type:

Figure 7: Risk Versus Return by Investment Type

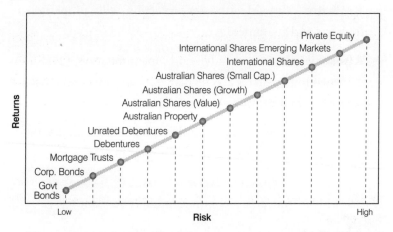

Note: This graph is used for illustration-only purposes, as one can argue Risk/Return ratings by segment forever.

Looking at this graph, we believe the best place to invest sits somewhere in the middle, with an educated mindset and a long-term approach. Sure, it's a lower risk profile but it doesn't have to mean lower wealth outcomes. Residential property is the perfect example which is why we recommend it!

What about Australia's investment habits? Who's doing it and where do you sit in comparison to every other investor? If we take a look at statistics from the Australian Tax Office (ATO), they show that the number of investors has been steadily increasing, which is great, as it shows they are prepared to take charge of their own destiny.

Figure 8: An increasing number of investors

Tax year	No. of investors	Yearly increase	% increase
2011–12	1,895,775	84,600	4.67%
2010–11	1,811,175	46,251	2.62%
2009–10	1,764,924	–	–

Source: ATO

However, if you take into account Australia's population – 23+ million – these are small numbers. The fact is, only a very small percentage of the population invests in property. According to the ATO, seven out of every ten property investors stop at making only one investment property, and only 2 and 1 per cent respectively buy four or five. Sure, buying just one property puts you in the investment market but the reality is you won't achieve a passive income from buying just one investment property.

Figure 9: Number of investors with one or more investment properties

Number of properties	Number of investors	Proportion
One	1,284,852	73%
Two	318,295	18%
Three	96,991	5%
Four	34,967	2%
Five	14,555	1%
Six or more	15,264	1%
Total	**1,764,924**	

Source: ATO

If you only need to buy three to five investment properties, then why isn't everyone doing it, and why do so many just stop at one? If we return to our original point – it's because it is daunting. It's also scary when you feel as though you're all alone and don't really have a formula to follow, or worse still the first property you bought was an investment lemon.

This is why we designed the A, B, C and D of property investment. We call it our Four Pillars of Property Investing formula. It's been created to give you a pathway towards that all-important first, second, third and fourth property purchase, and ultimately, true wealth creation.

Get all four right and you'll be well on your way to building what should be a straightforward property portfolio. If you get stuck – or even if you don't! – you can always connect with a range of industry savvy professionals, such as a qualified property investment adviser, a mortgage broker with a solid understanding of property investment structures as well as a good financial planner and buyer's agent.

THE PROPERTY INVESTMENT FORMULA 5

Now that you've got an understanding of the fundamentals of investing, you're ready to get to grips with you what we've fine-tuned over many years – our Four Pillars of Property Investing formula.

When it comes to buying an investment property, and particularly your first, it's a daunting process knowing what to do. It can be an exceptionally steep learning curve and it's hard to understand, collect and process all of the information out there that you feel you need. But you're off to an excellent start – you've got an understanding of the Five Essential Steps we covered in Part One of this book, as well as an appreciation of the mindset and psychology of investing.

After many years of working in the industry and advising hundreds of clients, we reckon our Four Pillars formula represents a fantastic opportunity for all budding property investors to know exactly what they need to master. It will allow you to create a passive income for life – using property as a vehicle. We share it with you in this book and you can implement the strategy with as few as three to five investment properties.

On the market right now are books that shout from the rooftops their ability to help you create a property empire: buy 100+ properties, 11 properties in 11 minutes and become rich the easy way. The simple fact is you just don't need to buy a score of properties in order to create a passive income for life and improve your wealth in the process. You don't even need the 10+ properties you might regularly read about. Instead, we think in most cases you actually only need three to five. That's right – three to five.

Let's delve into each of the Four Pillars.

A – Asset selection

Let's face it; this is the 'doing' part. It's what most people are interested in and it's what most people start with – the property. As we've outlined previously, property investment is a process not an event and there are a number of things to unpack when it comes to choosing a successful asset.

By asset selection, we are referring to bricks-and-mortar property and the process we work through to choose one over the other. For many of us, it's far easier – and more exciting – to inspect a property either in person or online rather than inspect the numbers. A physical inspection introduces a tangible element that numbers can't produce, and by this we mean you can actually 'see' your potential property investment face to face, and walk through it checking out all the nooks and crannies. But beware, this 'touch and feel' first approach has derailed many a property investor and is an urge that needs to be resisted. There is nothing more discouraging than seeing the look on a client's face when they realise they have bought the wrong asset and have to accept the related opportunity cost. It's made worse still because they can't get the lost years back!

In order to make informed asset selections, you need to understand the macro and micro implications of an investment. The macro relates to economics, and how economics is diversified and operates in a particular marketplace. For example, if you take a large, diversified city, such as London, New York or Tokyo, you'll need to understand the size of the marketplace as well as the attached scarcity value around the land, because this will then be affected by the human interest (lifestyle) and human behaviour (status) factors. The micro then takes a closer look at factors such as what makes for an investment-grade suburb, neighbourhood, street and finally the property itself, taking into account things like the floor plan, orientation, character and context to the norm in the area.

You probably think you're pretty good at choosing a property to live in for yourself, but what's difficult to acknowledge for the amateur investor is that buying a property to live in is simply a game of bricks and mortar. Buying a property to invest in is a game of finance – and there is a big difference – and the two are not to be confused. So the question is which one do you choose?

BRYCE's Tip

As I mentioned in my introduction, my very first investment was a property I purchased from the developer in the investment-grade Perth suburb of Victoria Park. At the time, I fell into the trap that I see now over and over again, where I was seduced by depreciation and the lifestyle amenities on offer – which included a pool, caretaker and lift – rather than the future value performance of the property. This was my first rookie mistake because after all, as the investor, I never got to use these facilities! Worse still, I was paying for the maintenance of the centralised lift that my property never even had access to! Upon reflection, this property has only made 5 per cent compound growth since purchase, which is an underperforming result for this location. My decision is made worse by knowing that other more investment-grade properties within the same suburb have outperformed this one during the same time period. Asset selection is therefore critical. However, I have no regrets as it was a great lesson to learn. Since this purchase, I now prefer to purchase established properties (personally and professionally) with no expensive amenities.

Location

For us, it's never about the property first. Successful asset selection is always about the location and we start with this and work backwards from macro to micro (see Figure 10). A good rule of thumb is that if you're investing for growth, 80 per cent of your return will come from the property's location and 20 per cent from the property. In other words, location does 80 per cent of the heavy lifting, and you get the cream from getting the property selection right.

Figure 10: Asset selection framework

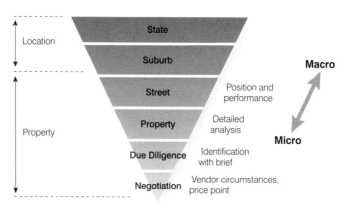

So your game plan should be to choose from:

→ **State** – Consider the larger area first and check out which state you can invest in. When you start at state level you are effectively researching each city within a state and the subsequent opportunity within that city. Interestingly, for optimal outcomes, this may not be your own state depending on where we currently are in the property cycle. Investors who simply choose their own state because they know it, may be trading opportunity for familiarity. Don't let 'good' be the thief of 'best'. Instead, consider being a borderless investor. Determine which state is currently either in (or soon to be in) the upturn phase of the property cycle if you're chasing growth or which state is offering desired rental yields if you're chasing income. The good news is that you don't need a crystal-ball to do this as history provides very useful guidelines to spot where you should be investing.

→ **Suburb** – Next, start getting into suburb selection. Look at things such as amenities, including schools, cafes, restaurants and other good lifestyle indicators. Also, just because it's in the next good suburb doesn't mean it's not a good investment. Importantly, not all suburbs are investment-grade. Choosing a suburb is all about demographics. By understanding who lives in a suburb we can determine the leading indicators that drive better growth and rental returns. It's about understanding the relationship between economic activity, human interest and human behaviour (more on that later).

→ **Street** – Now you're really fine-tuning your asset selection. This is where you'll need to consider things such as street appeal, liveability of the area, local amenities, consistency of housing stock, street parking, general overcrowding of too many dwellings, high side, low side, elevation, etc. In every suburb, there are the A-grade, B-grade as well as C-grade streets. We want to focus on the A and B grades as the C-grade streets will often have flaws that ultimately affect the performance of our investment.

 BRYCE's Food for Thought

Here are some interesting stats for you: there are 9.4 million dwellings in Australia, more than 15,000 suburbs and 2,500+ new properties coming onto the market each week. Not all suburbs are investment-grade, and of the investment-grade suburbs, not all of the properties in that suburb make a good investment. So the question for every investor is: which one should you buy?

Figure 11: Property numbers by states

Location of properties	No. of properties	Proportion
New South Wales	812,265	30%
Queensland	663,910	24%
Victoria	627,725	23%
Western Australia	305,240	11%
South Australia	178,650	7%
Australian Capital Territory	51,435	2%
Tasmania	49,060	2%
Northern Territory	26,150	1%
Total	**2,714,435**	

Source: ATO 2012

What Figure 11 shows is the popularity for property on the eastern seaboard of Australia. You might remember we discussed how important it is to consider opportunities outside your own backyard – being a borderless property investor – and these stats owe a great confirmation of this. Besides the obvious fact that the greater the population and density, the more diversified the economy, the sheer numbers here should give you comfort that there should be many opportunities out there – you just need to know where to look!

It's worth remembering that even if you get the location right but your asset isn't quite the best, you'll still benefit from the location factor. We call this the drag up effect. But there is an exception, and that's medium- or high-density accommodation. As there's inevitably going to be a far greater proliferation (supply) of accommodation in that particular area, the scarcity factor is lost, which in turn creates an underperforming asset return.

New vs old

The biggest mistake people make is getting distracted by what we call 'the bling'. This is typically reserved for brand new properties, whether it's an apartment in a boutique block or within a much larger development. These buyers get sold on the 'shine' of the stone bench-tops and the stainless steel appliances, and even things like the so-called depreciation. They are wowed by the sleek display suites, fancy brochures with 'headline' selling points and other distractions such as the five-star building amenities.

This is an inherent danger because what you're actually doing is buying the developer's profit line. Instead, you need to see the bigger picture behind the scenes which will really inform you as to the quality of that potential investment.

For example, two streets away, you might be presented with an 'established' two-bedroom apartment in a '70s block, that's still reliable and durable, for around $400,000. Up the street is a new shiny apartment block about to be completed with 'the bling'. They both have similar floor plans, the same internal floor size, yet the new one is selling for $150,000 more. In 20 years' time, they will both be considered 'old' so your best bet is to opt for the older of the two, which will have a better yield (rental) return. It will also benefit from the uplift in price growth that will occur as a result of the new apartments changing the median value of the area. The bottom line is you will receive a better investment return that we like to call an 'outperform' result.

Now, don't get us wrong. We will buy new if we feel the numbers stack up in terms of the price point. In any given year we'll probably negotiate on between 200 and 300 properties for our clients, and although this gives us a lot of insight into the market, it's actually very, very rare we'll find a new property that is truly investment-grade.

If we do find ourselves in a position to look for new stock, we'll be looking at these factors:

→ **Boutique.** Does it have the boutique/unique factors? It needs to be really scarce!

→ **Size of development.** If it's an apartment, is it a large or smaller development? Ideally, the smaller the better and we would prefer blocks of 12 or fewer wherever possible.

→ **Does it have its own title?** Has the block been subdivided into a number of different dwellings? Make sure you check with the agent what's included on the title – the back courtyard or the front car space are the most common grey areas.

Character

The location in which we buy will do most of the heavy lifting in terms of the capital growth return but you can also get an out-perform result based on the property type as well. You might be bang on with the location but tweak things a little by focusing on the property itself. By this we mean selecting a property with intrinsic character and period style. These properties have a real 'status' element to them that owner-occupiers love. They buy them with emotional hearts which pushes their values up beyond the normal range. These properties command attention due to the liveability factor of their interiors, from the floor plan, ceiling height and wide hallways to the kitchen or the courtyard, etc. They create an emotional bond in exactly the same way as some people are drawn to a classic cars or expensive artwork, for which they will pay a premium.

Asset selection summary

The take-home message here? Start with the big picture in mind, not the property. If faced with the choice between suburb vs property, always choose suburb first. It's the ONLY way you'll really understand how the property will likely perform. Start with the state, move on to the investment-grade suburb and then get down to street level. Don't get distracted by the shiny taps!

The tricky thing about developers

Before we move onto the second pillar, B, borrowing power, let's take a moment to consider developers. You can be forgiven for falling for new developments because developers have a big bag of tricks. Here are some of them.

Developer's trick #1

Make sure you don't get seduced by the allure of depreciation. This is often the number one sales tool that a selling agent will use to pique your interest; they will suggest that the potential investment is all about saving you some tax. But it's not; you don't get to pocket the tax refund each year to spend on your lifestyle but rather it goes towards the cash flow of the investment. The last thing you want is your 'treasured' tax savings servicing a lemon! If you're buying a property that could be compromised on things like scarcity or owner-occupier appeal just to get depreciation, you've taken your eye off the main game, i.e. the growth! Instead, you could consider a similar established property in a better area, and create the depreciation benefit instead of buying it – through a clever renovation.

Developer's trick #2

Project sales developers will also pressure you with slick talk about the holding costs. It goes something like this: "This is only going to cost you $50 a week to hold, once we factor in all this depreciation". Sounds good if the purse strings can afford it, but for many people adding 'only' an extra $20, $30 or $40 a week means you can alternatively hold an existing, established property and still get the benefit of capital growth plus a higher rental yield.

Developer's trick #3

Be wary of project marketers talking about the importance of land when selecting your investment property: "Land is what drives the price" is the common myth we hear being peddled. But here's the key to the message that is often critically overlooked – it's not about land "content", it's all about land "value". For example, let's say you've got $500,000 to spend on an investment property. You could buy a two-bedroom apartment 5 km from the CBD as one of a group of say 12 apartments. Sure, you won't be able to walk outside and say "that bit of land there is mine". But you will be able to say one-twelfth of the land footprint is mine, as well as the key lifestyle advantages of the local amenities on offer including the cafes, restaurants and bars, easy access to the public transport, popular schools as well as convenience stores around you.

Or, you could spend the same amount and buy a brand new house and land investment package which, for the same budget, is likely to be 20 km to 40 km from the CBD because you can't find a house for that price within the 5 km radius. The land-only disciples can be heard cheering, "well done" because after all you have land content in your investment. However, in our view the lifestyle drivers underpinning the land value closer to the CBD drive the performance of the asset – despite the fact that the land content is lower. If you are heading out to a greenfields estate and thinking you're getting more bang for your buck, you are, in our view, mistaken. This property's location will undermine the performance of your asset. Put simply, the percentage of the purchase price going towards the land for the apartment is higher and the percentage for the building is lower… while, critically, the opposite is true for the house and land package; the majority of the purchase price is towards the build and the lesser percentage towards the land. Ironic isn't it? Furthermore, you're not likely to attract the type of demographic who has the income growth potential that is required to push up the property values in that area. People who want the status and the recognition associated with the locations closer to the city will not buy in these areas, and hence the underperforming cycle or 'glass ceilings' will continue.

Developer's trick #4

Beware rental guarantees – these are wolves in sheep's clothing. Don't be persuaded by the idea that even if the property isn't let your rental income will be guaranteed for the first one or two years. The developers have built this into the price of the property. Furthermore, if it's such a great investment why do they need to give you a guarantee? If it is 'investment-grade', renters will be plentiful won't they?

B – Borrowing power

Now to our second pillar: whether you're a seasoned investor or just starting out, one of the key things you'll need to get your head around is having access to money – as we have been drumming into you throughout the earlier part of this book. This is because, quite simply, money is the vehicle to build your property investment portfolio. If you have borrowing power, i.e. the opportunity to borrow money when you want, this buys you the chance to put your portfolio into another gear. On the flipside, you could have great real estate, but if you get borrowing power wrong, you will hit your lending limit sooner than you would have hoped.

What do we mean by borrowing power?

Borrowing power is the combination of your income and surplus cash, and then seeing how much money you can borrow to acquire property. The idea is to have the smallest amount of your money and equity working to control the biggest property asset base, while at the same time not putting financial strain on the household. Get it right and you're well on your way to a very enjoyable retirement, but get it wrong and you're right back to square one.

Why is it so important?

Let's show you by way of an example. A client came to us a few years ago with a fantastic looking property portfolio. On paper it seemed great and the clients even had the ability to borrow more because they had equity in their property and really great income. The problem was that they had all of their lending – a couple of million dollars – with only one bank that decided they had too much exposure (money lent to that client). This bank decided that it wouldn't lend anymore, even though the clients could easily afford this extra borrowing. With no further borrowing power with that bank, they thought they could not continue to build their portfolio of properties. Yet with the help of our experienced mortgage brokers, we set about restructuring their lending with a couple of lenders and therefore they were able to add another property to their portfolio. That's just one example of why it's important to get appropriate professional advice.

How do you get borrowing power?

For the most part it will come down to one word – income. If you have regular, secure income, doors will open and you'll be able to build your property portfolio, so long as you can of course cover your costs of running your household. Other items that will impact borrowing power in a positive way are rental incomes, negative gearing and some depreciation add backs. On the negative side of the ledger are things such as credit card limits and personal or car loans with short-term life spans because the principal component that needs to be paid back in five years or less reduces borrowing power.

A good rule of thumb relating to borrowing power and household cash flow management is when you have lower incomes, it's best to look for properties with higher rental returns. Conversely, for higher incomes, then the focus should be on capital growth returns.

Leverage

We touched on this before, but it's important to talk about borrowing power as part of the story of leverage. A good way to think about leverage is to imagine it as an independent umpire deciding which asset class you should go into. You've got a few different choices, but let's just assume it comes down to either shares or property. For example, say you bought some shares offering a potential return of 12 or 13 per cent and you also bought real estate offering the potential of an 8 per cent return.

The shares look pretty good at face value but if you can leverage more into real estate, then that 8 per cent will give you a better dollar return than the 12 per cent from your shares. That's the beauty of leverage. We're not saying just choose real estate and exclude every other asset class but in the context of your borrowing power, leverage can provide a greater cash-on-cash return.

What's a cash-on-cash return?

As we outlined in Chapter 4, if you invest $100,000 for this simplistic example, to control an asset worth $500,000, then you're potentially magnifying your returns. Of course, there is a debt there of $400,000 but you're getting a faster cash-on-cash return. Instead of getting a return just on the $100,000 you are getting the return on the $500,000. If the return was say 5 per cent for each, then your $100,000 would make $5,000, but your $500,000 would make $25,000, (less the cost of your debt), but even then it's still significantly more than the $5,000 you made by only investing the smaller amount.

A little word of warning, leverage is great if used smartly and on asset classes that experience low volatility. Many thousands of people have lost small fortunes by leveraging into shares on the stock market. This is because stock values can fall sharply in a short period of time. These investors have not magnified their gains, they have magnified their losses – that's why we only like to see leverage used sensibly on investment-grade residential property (refer to Figure 5 on page 91).

Structure

Our message here with borrowing power is that we're not totally fixated on cheap interest rates and the lender's holding costs, which may sound a little unusual given these are the most obvious considerations when it comes to working with a bank to borrow money. We are more interested in firstly being able to secure the loan to invest and then it's all about the lending strategy and structure. Think about it like this: clever finance is more about the material gain you make through the leveraged asset, such as a 5 per cent gain on a $300,000 property – which is a $15,000 gain – rather than a straightforward material gain, such as saving $300 on having a cheaper interest rate. That $15,000 isn't exactly going to be sitting on your doorstep in cold hard cash, but too often people get caught up in the numbers that are easier to understand and more visual, which is a short-sighted mindset.

Of course, securing a competitive interest rate is important to us when we look after our clients. But securing the loan to invest first, and then ensuring we can set up our Money SMARTS structure, takes priority for us and will see our clients achieve much bigger financial gains later on. If you can set up your finance in the most effective way, you'll find it quite straightforward to build your portfolio. Finance for us is a bit like a game of chess – you always need to be thinking a few moves ahead. Building a property portfolio is the same – you need to be thinking one to two loans in advance. As we mentioned, it's not about interest rates and establishment costs, it's all about structure.

The key is to find a banker or finance professional who's aware of things such as cross-securitisation or cross-collateralisation, because not every banker will show you the right way to do things. It may be better to work with an investment-savvy mortgage broker who understands structure and can also talk to numerous lenders to help you set up your portfolio.

The Great Australian Dream

Often talked about in the media, as well as around the barbecue, the Great Australian Dream is one of those golden concepts that continues to hold sway in property circles. The media loves it because it's nostalgic and harks back to an era of Hills Hoists and quarter acre blocks. The reality is that today, however, younger generations want different things. So many of the sitcoms watched by Gen Ys focus on apartment living rather than big country homesteads that they've developed a different appetite for what represents their own Great Australian Dream.

Let's back track to give this some context: Australia was a young nation during World War II. When our soldiers began returning home, it kick started a boom period that extended into the '50s and '60s, when we were living relatively well with plenty of manufacturing jobs and a high standard of living. In contrast to the Great Depression of the early 1930s, where only 30 per cent of people owned their own home, these later years saw many Australians begin to think they could own their own home too. Of course, the suburbs and suburban houses were born and the Great Australian Dream took flight, with bricks and mortar being built and snapped up all over the country. It was also during this time that we could see a very strong correlation between household disposable income and borrowing power to the value of the property.

During the '70s we started to see a swing. Stay-at-home mothers were working in part-time jobs, which bolstered household income, and many women were also embarking on full-time careers, which continued through to the '90s. Then the "recession we had to have" hit us, and the economy suffered significantly. We got through those hard years of high interest rates and high inflation rates to become a more efficient and streamlined nation today, and we've grown and developed as a nation across the board. Nowadays, it's common for our households to comprise double incomes, vastly increasing the household's total disposable income, and along with the ability to source lower interest rates, the opportunity is there to borrow more, pushing property values higher.

The message here is that when interest rates are low, borrowing power increases. Money was accessible during the boom times because the jobs and infrastructure were there, but everything ground to a halt during the '90s recession. Today, we are enjoying low interest rates again, which act as a lever to push property prices higher. We talk about this as being the 'rising tide lifting all ships'.

 *BEN's Case Study*

This case study is about a couple buying their first home. It documents the relationship between prices and borrowing power. Our young couple heads off to see their mortgage broker already with a bit of an idea as to what they want to spend on a house. They've done their budget and it's around the $500,000 mark. The broker crunches some numbers to do with their income, cash flow and lifestyle and presents some options. Suddenly, it seems as though some of the lenders will loan up to $550,000. But the couple only wants to borrow $460,000 and use some of their savings to complete the purchase. Armed with that knowledge, they leave, hit the websites and start searching for properties they think are worth the lower amount. Once they start attending open for inspections, they realise their $500,000 doesn't get them much. Further, because agents never advertise the actual value of a property (typically they list a price 20 per cent or more below the reserve), our couple finds themselves conditioned to look at properties with a higher price. That higher price has now become their new budget, because firstly they justify to themselves they will get more 'home' if they spend more, and secondly other buyers have higher borrowing power as interest rates are lower, which forces the value of property higher. Make sense?

Looking into the future, when we won't be at these historically low interest rates, we need to look at other growth drivers that may impact property values, because household incomes will have hit their peaks. Therefore, we need to drill down into the suburb levels to find what's happening with incomes and how that is impacting prices. On a macro level, the rising tide that has lifted property values will stop when interest rates do eventually go up, yet we need to keep focusing on getting the best returns from the properties we buy. So borrowing power is the science of using other people's money and seeing what people can afford in particular marketplaces as we're studying different growth markets.

Borrowing power summary

To wrap up this discussion on borrowing power, it's about sensible gearing. It's about understanding what you can afford first, establishing what price point you should then be searching for, and then finding the asset that best complements your price.

To help you, your options are either to go to a mortgage broker or to a bank. Be careful, you don't want to get yourself into a situation like the story we told earlier on about the client who had all of their loans with one bank. That situation would not have occurred had they had an investment-savvy mortgage broker. Get your team right and you'll be on the right track.

C – Cash flow management

This is possibly the hardest part of the Four Pillars property formula to get right, because good (and great) money management all starts with cash flow. If you can harness it correctly, it'll allow you to trap the surplus in your budget to really help you on your path to wealth creation and successful investment. It's the real cornerstone of what we do, and we are passionate about helping you become good cash flow managers because without surplus cash flow you can never invest, period!

We've already shown you our tried and tested techniques to help you get your household money under control (through our Money SMARTS accounts system), and it involves a fair amount of planning, observation and discipline. There's plenty of software around that you can tap into because there's nothing worse than going to all the trouble of creating a plan only to stick with it for a few months and then get sick of it without waiting to reap the reward.

Your advisers can only take you so far. They can indicate where you're at in terms of your household money and cash flow, but ultimately the hard work needs to come from you, because only you will know the actual numbers required to make the whole system work. Added to this is that everyone has different ideas of what constitutes cash flow management.

However, if you're on the right path with step C in the Four Pillars formula you should already have factored in all of the components of your household budget. This means you're ready to take into account your next step: how much an investment property is actually going to cost you each year.

That's the challenge – bringing together your household money and the investment property cost, and getting the two to talk. While we've been doing exactly that for not only our clients but also ourselves over the past few decades, in our experience the ability to get these two components to mesh is actually the really hard part.

This is why: it's because you need to combine them together. You need to be able to combine things such as a kitchen renovation, paying for school fees and even how you're going to be able to take an annual holiday, as well as cover the interest costs and pay the rates on your investment property.

The good news is that it's fairly simple to achieve a level of good money management once you've got your head around the planning and tracking required. So let's consider a few advanced approaches to help you on the path to effective money management.

Good money management

Let's look at what is considered good money management. This is where you reconcile and measure every single dollar that you spend against your bank account statement at the end of each month. That means every dollar! This really is the most fundamental step in understanding where your money goes, but it takes some practice to set aside the time to actually do it. We do it ourselves every month and you should too.

The good news here is that by just being a good money manager you will vastly improve your chances of achieving a self funded retirement, so long as you still follow the four A, B, C and D principles of the Four Pillars.

Great money management

This is where you take the information from your monthly reconciliation and forward project it. You forward allocate your money into the future, allowing you to set it aside to use for wealth creation. This is advanced, or what we call great, money management. You are like a true financial controller of your money and household. This means factoring in projections, variables and forecasts for future money events, as well as taking into account periods over the next few years that might be affected by less money generating activities, such as taking maternity leave or coping with a redundancy. We're talking a little about 'defence' here, our next pillar, but great money management is about looking at your budget and projecting it into the future, taking into account all the things that can pop up.

How do you do it?

If you return to our very first chapter on mindset, this is where you must begin in order to effect change. We need you to think about your views on money, the views handed down to you by your parents or guardians, and previous generations, and get them in check. We've already talked about how running a household is like running a business, and that's what we keep returning to. When you think about it, a CEO of a large company wouldn't run their business without a complete set of budgets, forecasts, cash flow provisions, etc. supplied by the financial controller in what is referred to as a cash flow modelling simulator. They use this simulator to run models and business scenarios and they certainly wouldn't be making big decisions without this data and the insight it gives them. It involves you changing your mindset to realise you can do it too and then building yourself a simulator (spreadsheet) to model future events.

The reason why we do this is pretty simple really – you can work out the very best application of your money to get you the very best returns. Having the data and insight at your fingertips means you make wiser decisions and put your money to work harder to achieve superior returns.

We've given you the frameworks, templates and resources to help you break cash flow management down and make it easier to roll out, and with a bit of faith in yourself you can become a great manager too. If we take away the complexity and layers surrounding money, and bring it back to basic principles, then the world will be your oyster. You just have to get your mindset right and think like a CEO. We talk more about 'great' money management later in the book – look out for the money and wealth accumulation model in Chapter 10 (page 219).

BRYCE's Tip

If we think about how our grandparents managed money, life was a lot simpler, wasn't it? They had a jar for housekeeping, a jar for bills and a jar for savings. Fast forward to today, and the biggest threat is those little plastic cards that enable cash withdrawals on demand. Then add into the mix credit cards using money that isn't even ours, and it's easy to see how household budgets spiral out of control. We talk about how to use credit cards to your advantage in our Money SMARTS section, but the key message is that good and great money management starts with your cash flow and running future scenarios.

Step 1: What are our sources of money?

The first step to effective cash flow management is to take you back to the start – where does your money come from? At its most fundamental level, everyone has different avenues for earning money, whether that's as a self-employed employee, or a PAYG wage-earner, as Figure 12 displays.

FIGURE 12: Flow of money

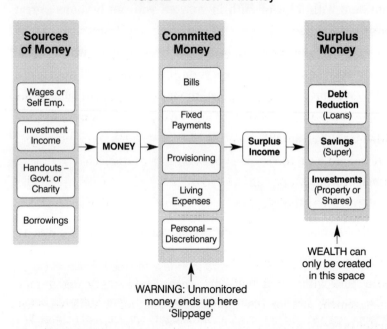

Your committed money is where your money goes, which might be to your bills, payments and other provisioning. But it's also where the unmonitored spending occurs, and where you are most likely to run into problems because it takes into account your living, lifestyle and discretionary spending.

Tracking the money that's left over – your SURPLUS income – is the aim of the whole exercise. Ultimately what you do with this money will determine your level of wealth in later life. It's that simple. If the surplus doesn't materialise, i.e. it's spent before you get access to it, well the show's over ladies and gentlemen and there's little hope that you will build any wealth. Pray for the lotto win or getting some of Uncle Frank's inheritance because you won't be in a position to create it yourself!

Step 2: Budgets

Here's the funny thing about budgets – they simply don't work alone! If you really think about it, a budget is typically retrospective. It takes into account your past or present financial situation, without looking ahead to the future. It is a static look at money and cash flow. As soon as something comes along to derail it, your budget gets left behind and you're right back at square one. That's why we developed our Money SMARTS system, so Step 2 is to replace the need for a static budget and start thinking about allowances which we talk about in Step 4.

Step 3: Cash flow simulation

So it's out with the static budget and in with the 'great' money management solution of forward projecting your cash flows. What better peace of mind is there than knowing you have worked the numbers and you are confident you can afford to invest and not stress out about the household finances? Assess incomes and expenditure on a monthly or yearly basis and realise your potential.

If you are planning to go down to one income or salary, you might have thought initially you'd have to sell an investment property to free up some cash flow, because in one way you are in a negative cash flow position for a period of nine months (or however long you take maternity leave). But by building a cash flow simulator you have realised that using your line of credit for this short period means you can hang onto that property now. Sure, you will pay for the privilege of using borrowed money to give yourself cash during this short period, but your property will still be in your portfolio and will continue to deliver you strong returns for the current year and years ahead. Surely that justifies your position in doing it in the first instance and you will be financially better off. Thank you cash flow simulator!

Step 4: Modernising the jar system (allowances)

Society has made money complex when it doesn't have to be. If you can essentially go back to your grandparent's jar system, it should be very simple.

Given you are using 'good' or 'great' money management assessments now, and you have adopted the Money SMARTS system, you will be able to work out what money allowance you need for what things each week.

→ Flour Jar 1 – Living and Lifestyle Account – Visa or Mastercard debit card

→ Flour Jar 2 – Primary Account (offset account)

→ Flour Jar 3 – 55-day interest-free Credit Card Account

See? It's not that hard really.

Remember, if you can foresee that your earning capacity will decrease in the short term, the trick is not to panic and act from a position of weakness. As we've shown, it's possible to trade your way through a tricky patch and end up better over the long run.

If you're not confident to act from a position of strength – seek out advice and let someone give you all the options based on the figures NOT an opinion.

BEN's Tip

Interest rates today are at the lowest they've been for more than 60 years. This means you should be stress-testing your cash flow models to ensure that you will still be OK if rates were higher than they are now. If they do rise – and inevitably they will – you might suddenly have a bigger monthly outlay, so it pays to do the maths beforehand to protect your cash flow reserves. Perhaps if the rates go up, you won't be able to afford some of the finer things in life you're currently enjoying. Even a modest increase could put your monthly budget under pressure. In some instances, locking a portion of your lending into a fixed position can help you better protect yourself, but remember it's still important to have some flexibility and cash flow buffers.

D – Defence

The final Pillar is 'defence'. While everyone loves asset selection, the love is not so widespread for defence. That's because while the investor is usually so consumed by the accumulation of the assets, they often don't realise that they themselves are actually the most important asset.

The easiest way to think about this last pillar of defence is with another word – protection. So defence is all about protecting two things: one, the property asset, which could be covered by taking out building and landlord's protection insurance; and two, protecting *you*, the income generator.

Put simply the 'D' for defence is crucial. We went into a little bit of detail about this in Part One, but this section is actually more the domain of an experienced financial planner who is licensed to give you this sort of advice and can help you set up the relevant insurances to protect your income and your lifestyle. Insurances you need to consider are life insurance, income protection insurance, and total or permanent disability insurance. When you're an investor you need to look at insurance like this: it is an asset and I'm paying for an asset that in reality I never really want to cash in, as it means I've got a health problem or my property has a problem.

What we do want to leave you with is this: if you go to the effort of creating a well-defined and well-performing property portfolio without the right defence in place, you're really leaving yourself vulnerable to outside influences that could have a very serious impact on your future wealth you had done so well in planning for. If your income stops then so does this investment strategy, given leverage is involved.

BRYCE's Case Study

I received an email that went like this: "About three years ago, a colleague developed MS (multiple sclerosis) and hasn't worked since. As a result, I sorted my stuff out and increased my super, bolstered my life insurance and TPD (total and permanent disability) insurance and got a solicitor to draft up a will. I also took out IP (income protection) insurance. Had the above not happened to the colleague at work, I don't think I would have done it. Then seven weeks ago I was diagnosed with cancer. Fortunately, post a few surgeries and now undergoing chemo, things will hopefully be OK. My message is that the D step is critical. It's a hard sell as I was one of those ones who said it would never happen to me. But illness doesn't discriminate, it can happen to anyone."

A team to bring it all together

Now you have what we believe are the key formulas required in order to start to build your property portfolio. We've covered the four essential elements to the Four Pillars Property Investment Formula: Asset selection, Borrowing power, Cash flow management and Defence, as well as the Five Essential Steps: Clarify, Evaluate, Plan, Implement and Manage.

The ball's in your court if you want to be a DIY exponent of this knowledge, now that you have a greater understanding of it. However, if you think that you are going to need some help, we've also shown you the four major players in the industry, so you can understand whether you want to go down the free or fee-based model. Wouldn't it be great if there were a specialist in the marketplace who was able to bring all of these together? This challenge is near impossible in terms of being able to find someone who is formally qualified in all these areas, and if you do find someone the other big challenge is how does this professional keep up with all the latest developments and changes across such a broad range of disciplines?

The likely scenario is that you won't find such a person readily available in your area, so your next best option is to look for a specialist who provides property investment advice and then look to see what other services they offer to help you build your investment team.

If you are looking to hand-select each professional specialist, just be mindful that they all might have their own opinion on each other's area of expertise. All of them will also have an opinion about property investment, so again be prepared for differing views if you try to build your own team.

If you are looking for a one-stop-shop approach, just make sure you revisit how the professionals in their team are paid – see Chapter 3 – and ensure that they don't have any conflicts of interest in the advisory work they do.

Your best approach is to bring an advisory team together that is working for your best interests and allows you to build a portfolio conservatively and comfortably to help you achieve your goals.

Property investment adviser

The very best person to talk to first is a property investment adviser who is formally educated to advise others e.g. a Qualified Property Investment Adviser (QPIA). Your professional adviser is responsible for working with you to develop a property wealth plan. Your property wealth plan will consist of information about:

→ Your personal goals – (Clarify)

→ Your property investment goals – (Clarify)

→ Your overall retirement target – (Clarify and Evaluate)

→ Your risk assessment – (Clarify and Evaluate)

→ Your current financial position – (Clarify and Evaluate)

→ Their recommended property investment strategy or strategies (Plan and Implement, A – Asset Selection, C – Cash flow)

→ Their recommended property purchases (Plan, Implement, Asset Selection, Cash flow, Borrowings)

→ Financial information about any property recommendation (Plan, Implement, Cash flow, Borrowings)

→ Property portfolio modelling (including cash flow models for each property)

→ Financial information about your total property portfolio (Implementation, Manage)

→ If they are working with other qualified professionals, such as a mortgage adviser, the information about your loan structures and lending (Plan, Implement, Manage, Cash flow, Borrowings)

→ If they are working with a buyer's agent, or your adviser is a buyer's agent him or herself, then they can also help implement this plan by securing the investment property recommended within the plan (Implementation, Asset Selection)

→ If they are working with a financial planner, then expect to receive a separate document called a Statement of Advice – (Implement, Manage, Cash flow, Defence) and detailed cash flow projections – (Implement, Manage, Cash flow, Plan). Their plans should be written with extensive detail, because they are effectively playing with your financial future, so you have a right to know and understand everything within them.

Other advisers

A buyers' agent will work with you to find and buy the very best assets in the investment-grade suburbs, which will help you to achieve your passive income goals.

Investment-savvy mortgage brokers are advisers who not only understand finance, as in interest rates and establishment costs, but also structure. A good mortgage broker will not just be thinking about you buying one investment property, but also thinking about you buying the second and third – a bit like a game of chess. They should also be competent enough to do detailed cash flow modelling for you.

Financial planners. Our tip is to find a planner who is skilled in strategy, because without a short- and long-term strategy, it's much harder to consider the bigger picture about where you are going and what you want to achieve. Your financial planner is also potentially going to be responsible for your superannuation or SMSF returns, which will form part of your overall wealth position and include your property investment portfolio. They should also be able to assist with cash flow modelling.

Accountants will be responsible for ensuring your tax outcomes. They will make sure you are legally claiming all the deductions you are entitled too and do any tax planning with you. If you are buying in an SMSF, they will play a role in the administration of the fund. They should also be able to assist with cash flow modelling.

Conveyancers/solicitors. They are responsible for the review of any property sales contracts and also the settlement of purchases, by way of legally transferring the title of the property into your name. They are also there to review any other legal matters if they arise.

Property managers. Your investment properties are going to be some of your most expensive assets and the tenants you place in your properties are going to be very important selections. If you get the wrong tenant, you could be in for a difficult ride. We don't think it's wise to self-manage your property investments as there are lots of rules and regulation within tenancy acts around the country. Best to leave it to the professionals, we think!

These are the key advisers you'll need in order to build your investment portfolio. It's our experience that the best results come from ensuring that all of these areas of professional support are considered and catered for. Without this support, you're much more likely to run into trouble down the track.

THE PSYCHE BEHIND THE PRICE

6

In this chapter, we want to go further into the property side of things. You've already grasped the Five Essential Steps as well as the Property Investment Formula, which are key philosophies and action plans that we practise every day with our clients. You've learned about how the industry works and the best team of professionals that you can have to help you on your way to earning a debt-free income.

Here, we want to show you the science behind what makes an 'investment-grade' property. We've mentioned this phrase a few times already, but it's important for you to understand what we mean by it. To grade a location and then a property as 'investment-grade' requires in-depth research, assessment and a true understanding of value drivers within each property market. There are so many variables that influence property values, and it's incredible how many people get this wrong.

In this chapter, we'll get under the layers of property and share with you how the science and psychology of investing can influence prices and have done so for many, many years. It's knowledge we've learnt over a long period of time, helping many clients, and it's our hope that by sharing this with you you'll be better equipped to make more informed property investment decisions.

What do we mean by the science behind investing in property and how does it affect prices?

One of the great aspects we love about property is that it's bricks and mortar. It's tangible. You can see it, touch and control it, as you own it outright. We've said before that we favour property over all of the other asset classes because we believe over the long term it is the best vehicle for sustained wealth creation. We don't mean click your fingers and watch the cash roll in; we are talking about long-term, sustained and healthy wealth creation for passive rental income returns.

It's one thing to grab the paper on the weekend and look at properties that tick a few boxes, but it's quite another to actually understand why a property is priced a certain way and make a decision as to whether it will be investment-grade.

To examine the various market mechanisms, we'll first consider the supply and demand side of the conversation, and then the critical data indicators underlying both when it comes to investing.

Supply

This is all about making the right decision based on the land and accommodation stock available. In the land category, your first option is to buy vacant land, i.e. farmland. If there's lots of available land then it stands to reason that there's no shortage of supply. We could also assume that the farmland might eventually be rezoned into residential, with potential for further development, so you'd need to think about how that might limit the growth in value that you're going to enjoy from that investment.

FIGURE 13: Supply

 = Land and Accommodation Stock

The second most common land supply is the availability of possible subdivisions. This is about looking at what's around now and then looking at that longer-term availability.

If we move away from land stock towards accommodation, we start to talk about property household types. Besides stand-alone dwellings, we can also consider the current availability of high-rise accommodation, usually apartments. Any discussion about zoning or high-density property and thousands of new apartments being built, always comes with questions of oversupply. This is often an ongoing issue, particularly in Australia's CBDs, where prices can be affected by too much accommodation in one location.

Below is a list of critical supply considerations you need to consider:

→   Existing availability of vacant land

→   Future availability of possible subdivisions to enter market

→   Current availability of accommodation (by property household types – sale and rent)

→ Future availability (planning approval of stock to enter market by property household type)

→ Lead time and speed at which accommodation can be established.

What can you do about oversupply?

First, you can check the future availability of accommodation by working out where the planning approvals have been granted. This will enable you to predict the availability of supply that's coming onto the market. Second, you can also consider the lead time and speed at which the new accommodation will come onto the market. There are many factors that can influence when a product will hit the market. For example, bad weather conditions or poor sales campaigns can delay new property releases, so it's important to understand the forces that affect the supply and in turn affect your opportunity to get a good result. In summary, a high level of supply will impact negatively on a property's value. If supply is limited, this could be a good thing for values if demand exists.

Demand

By demand, we mean 'true' demand – the ability of owner-occupiers to realistically afford what they desire. In other words, their desire to get in and stay in a particular area and their ability to afford the accommodation (see Figure 14).

What we don't want are the opposite – the dreamers who have a genuine desire for the property but can't afford the prices. There are plenty of them; they're the ones looking at and falling in love with properties on the real estate websites, but they don't have the resources to buy this accommodation. We don't want to concern ourselves with this group because we don't see this as true enquiry, or true demand.

FIGURE 14: True Demand

= Want and Can Afford

True Demand = Desire to 'Get in' and 'Stay' (Area) and Ability to Afford (Accommodation) from an Owner Occupier Perspective

Let's unpack this a little further. From an analysis perspective, true demand translates as a combination of three key factors. These are all on our checklist when we're studying a new location or area to invest in.

1. Economic activity

This is the first thing to consider. What is the broader economic activity and what shape is it in at the time? Essentially, where do people get their jobs and how likely are those jobs to be secure?

2. Human behaviour

This is about getting into the psyche of the buyer. In our case, we're more interested in the psyche of owner-occupiers because they buy on emotion and desire (i.e. with their heart), as opposed to the investor who's investing for a return (i.e. with their calculator). Delving a little deeper, this is about image and the way property represents us and who we are. It includes factors such as:

→ **Status.** Buyers can be attracted to properties in blue chip areas so that they will be perceived as successful.

→ **Stigma.** An area might have an associated stigma because it attracts crime and a lower socio demographic, and this can put off buyers.

3. Human interest

Smart investors ride on the coat-tails of owner-occupiers who want to live in a particular location, because that's where they're going to enjoy longer, sustained returns, as opposed to returns on riskier ventures which experience boom and bust-type cycles. When we talk about human interest, we want to know about all the things that make an area a pleasure to live in. Commonly, these are:

→ Demographic profile and suburb status

→ Lifestyle and amenities

→ Access to public transport and/or good transport nodes

→ Proximity to the CBD, shopping strips or centres, restaurants, cafes, bars

→ Proximity to the beach

→ School zone inclusion, which is attractive to families.

All of this can be tricky to decipher. You might have a great understanding of these three key factors in your local area but have no idea about the same thing in other parts of Australia. Of course, the risk is that you buy a dud, under-performing property because you failed to consider the psychology behind the price.

In summary, the more demand you have, the higher the likely rate of value growth of the property. The lower the demand, usually the lower rate of growth in value.

BRYCE's Tip

I'm often asked for my opinion on how the 'property market' is going. I think generalised commentary on property in Australia is largely irrelevant because ultimately you're not buying 'the market', rather a single property in a localised market with localised conditions. Therefore, one of the biggest mistakes you can make is thinking that Australia is simply one big market. It's not; it's actually made up of hundreds and hundreds of sub-markets, each with its own intricacies. At any one time, each is operating within different phases of the property cycle, based on a wide range of factors. Experienced property investors will identify this and become what we recommend and have talked about before, i.e. 'borderless investors'. They make the most of buying counter-cyclically and therefore get optimal results for their portfolio. A word of caution though, interstate investing is not something you should take on lightly. If you're not confident in your knowledge and experience, then it's best to start working with an experienced and qualified professional like a buyer's agent.

BEN's Tip

Don't fall into the trap of searching for a property on the internet and thinking that this constitutes solid research. Searching is simply that – looking. It doesn't take into account the factors we're examining in depth here, which aren't going to be included in the property description online or in the glossy flyer the agent gives you. One of the best ways to do your research is to actually hit the streets and check out the property physically. Sure, go to the open for inspection but go back and really start hunting around. It's not until you're in the street – especially if you're unfamiliar with it – that you get a sense of the surrounding area. If you're not in the property itself, you won't see the huge towering apartment block next door. Furthermore, research is the key to keeping calm during the house-hunting process. See as many properties as you can in your price bracket (keeping in mind that property prices are usually listed 20 per cent below the reserve) and find out the sale prices achieved for comparable properties. A good rule of thumb is to complete a spreadsheet that tracks how quickly these properties are selling and if you can, record their selling price relative to the asking price.

Property indicators

Once you've got an understanding of how supply and demand work, you are ready to consider the three different types of property indicators. These are crucial when it comes to your decision-making on a property, as they are the real drivers of property and they give you a true indication of how a property will perform.

The three key indicators are:

1. **Marketplace indicators:** These indicators measure market activity

2. **Demographic indicators:** These look at profiling factors

3. **Human nature indicators:** These measure human interest and human behaviour.

You will also need to consider and work through each of the three key areas we identified earlier in this chapter (economic activity, human behaviour and human interest) and work out how they tie

THE PSYCHE BEHIND THE PRICE

in with the three indicators listed above. It's important to understand what you need to be looking at in order to create an outperforming result.

Marketplace indicators

Marketplace indicators are represented by lead and lag indicators, which you may have heard of.

Lead indicators are the measurable market performance factors that will tell you whether a property investment represents a good opportunity. They're crucial because they help predict and anticipate activity before a trend emerges. Taking the time to consider them all can make or break a property decision. While they might not all apply to every property you're considering, it's important to work through each of them in order to make an informed decision. These are some of the key lead indicators:

- → Stock on market
- → Stock for rent
- → Property search portals – area searches
- → Auction clearance rates
- → Planning approvals
- → Infrastructure approvals
- → Vacancy rates: sourced from property search portals such as Realestate.com.au or Domain.com.au
- → Days on the market.

Lag indicators are the statistics and figures that you'll see reported most in the media. The problem is that these stats represent what's gone on in the past, and so they lack the currency of leading indicators. The key lag indicators to watch out for include:

→ Median values reported

→ Vacancy rates: as a lagging indicator, vacancy rates rely on industry reporting, and are commonly two to three months old before they're released. The outcome is that you receive a false impression of the market

→ Financing activity: this falls into a similar category as vacancy rates because the RBA and the ABS delay the release of their stats on financing activity.

How does this apply to me?

These are all facts and figures you can obtain yourself. We suggest not tuning into the media as such, because they have an agenda to sell their platform, but instead going straight to the source. For example, you might like to create a spreadsheet tracking all of these details on properties that you think could make investment-grade. Search portals such as Realestate.com.au and Domain.com.au are getting better at publishing property data. Other great information and data sources include: CoreLogic RP data and their Property Value internet platform. Good sources of on-the-ground information include that provided by valuation firms Herron Todd White (monthly reports) and Charter Keck Kramer, as well as national property investment monthly publications such as *Australian Property Investor* and *Your Investment Property* magazines, the online *Smart Property Investment* website and the broader personal finance *Money* magazine.

Demographic indicators

Next up are demographic indicators. Simply put, the most powerful component that drives value is people's ability to afford it. So the following profiling factors – which take into account income, age and education mix – all play a part in the income component required to achieve an outperforming result when you locate areas and properties:

→ Suburb/LGA (local government area) household incomes and ages

→ Suburb/LGA education and occupation mix

→ Lifestyle and transport amenities

→ Employment and income prospects (short and long term)

→ Access and speed to mass employment centre(s). By this we mean the property's proximity to the area's larger employment centres. For example, distance to the CBD in your capital city

→ Education facilities. We often hear on the news about areas that have significantly increased in value because they're in a premium school zone. In some cases, schools tighten up their boundaries to include only one side of the street in the zone, which can lead to an increase in prices on that side

→ Localised population forecasts. What's going to happen to that area?

How does this apply to me?

The best source for demographic indicators is the Australia Bureau of Statistics (ABS). The ABS website, www.abs.gov.au, is fairly easy to navigate and you'll be able to find the most incredible array of statistics to help you in your search. You could also try logging on to the local newspaper online to get a sense of what's happening in specific neighbourhoods, as it relates to development or schools. Another great source is .id, (http://home.id.com.au) a company that forecasts populations and profiles demographics.

Human nature indicators

Once you've pinpointed your marketplace and demographic indicators, your final key piece of analysis are human nature indicators. We've already talked about this a little as it relates to 'supply and demand', but these are incredibly important indicators that we believe are some of the most crucial drivers of value.

To recap human behaviour, you want to look at the psyche of the owner-occupier. As we noted earlier, human behaviour is all about establishing the perceived image and the way a property is presented to reveal who we are.

There also needs to be human interest. What is it about the area that makes it enjoyable to live in?

How does this apply to me?

Human behaviour is the trickiest of the three data indicators to really pin down. For status and location, you could search for these in Google Earth to assess and isolate particular areas. For everything else we'd suggest using the 'Walk Score' sites and other ranking sites for restaurants and coffee shops, etc. (Sites like walkscore.com.au measure an amenity within walking distance of the actual property and rank that score. A high score means it has a great amount of amenities close by.) A hint is to work outwards from the CBD, as all the best infrastructure is usually located close to the major employment and activity centres in our cities. Then it comes down to good old-fashioned research, such as local papers (they are usually online these days) and also council reports and government planning reports.

BRYCE's Tips

Your returns are really governed by the area in which you buy. As a general rule, we think it's an 80/20 split, where 80 per cent of the return is derived from the area you buy in and 20 per cent comes from the property itself. There are exceptions where if you buy a property with really strong owner-occupier appeal then the property itself will deliver improved returns over and above this 80/20 split. These characteristics include its actual physical location, its period charm, internal features, floor plan, views or size, aspect, natural light, etc. At the other end of the scale, the property could result in a worse performance comparative to its area. This is usually a result of buying in a medium- or high-density development where there's no scarcity or owner-occupier appeal for the property type. As for location, we don't need to just look in our own backyard, we need to look around the country.

Don't get fooled by the bling and the shiny! That's not where the action's at. Remember that those types of new properties are at the higher end of the price range and typically it's the 'ugly ducklings' – the reliable and durable properties – that actually outperform from an investment perspective. In 20 years, that brand new property is going to be an old property just like the 40-year-old properties. They don't call it location, location, location for nothing!

Interestingly, we do like some medium-density areas that have been coming onto the market. You only need to check out train stations around Melbourne right now to see plenty of three- to five-storey apartment developments under construction. While we won't be buying into these complexes, the increased population is a perfect indicator of the future growth of the area, and the increased population will in itself create a flow-on for new lifestyle components, such as bars, cafes and restaurants to enable it to become an even more attractive area.

A story of two houses

This is a great example of what can happen when there's a house in two different locations built by the same builder. During the gold rush of the 1860s, Melbourne was a hotbed for development and activity. The proliferation of gold meant that stately houses started to spring up and create traditional blue-chip inner areas, such as Toorak, Camberwell, Hawthorn, Kew and Canterbury, etc., as well as further out in Victoria throughout regional townships including Ballarat, Bendigo and Castlemaine. If you take the argument that properties themselves are where the returns are, then why is it that in Castlemaine and Bendigo those properties now range from $800,000 to $1m to buy, whereas the same properties in the inner suburbs of Melbourne can range from between $5m to $8m? They were built at the same time, with the same craftsmanship and style. This example serves as strong evidence that it's not just about the acquisition of the actual property itself – it's about the location that it's in.

 BRYCE's Apartment Investment Tips

Not all apartments make the best investments and you need to be careful about choosing which one's right for you. Whether you're a fan of the Great Australian 'Quarter Acre Block' dream or you grew up thinking apartments were the norm, the truth is that there's no right or wrong – you just need to understand what makes for a good apartment investment as opposed to a mediocre one. So here it is.

We prefer established apartments over new. Preferably 1970s style but also 1930s Art Deco to 1950s and 1960s 'flats', because they usually have a better position, are surrounded by great homes and enjoy the lifestyle factor in spades.

Something new and shiny might have all the bells and whistles but at the end of the day it's your tenant who's going to use the facilities not you. Your money is more likely to be funnelled into the upkeep of these spaces through the owner's or body corporation fees.

Choose to invest in the land value rather than the building. You can achieve this by buying established stock because it typically offers more land-to-asset ratio and therefore more bang for your buck.

Established apartments are also preferred because you can peek into the property's past and check out its previous sales history to see what it has actually achieved rather than guessing, which you can't do for a brand new building. After all, we are investing not speculating!

As you can see, there are many, many factors that are involved in understanding the property indicators. But if we're to leave you with a final thought on pricing as a property investor – **it's better to be a price-taker than a price-maker.** What we mean by that is to let owner occupiers set the price, and investors take it, by getting the drag up value that's occurring in the location. Essentially you get sucked along for the ride! It only ends badly when it's around the other way – just look at mining town results recently to see this in action.

Next up, we're ready to get into the headspace of the buyer – that's you. We'll show you what you're doing right or wrong so that you can be ready to learn the strategies needed to pick a winning investment!

Summary so far...

✓ Property Market Mechanism

✓ Building your Team

✓ The Property Investment Formula

✓ Investment Foundations

✓ Industry Players

✓ Money SMARTS

✓ The Five Essential Steps

✓ The Four Foundation Levers

✓ Money Mindset

✓ Personal Values and Goals

A BUYER'S DECISION QUADRANT

7

I n Part Two we've spent a lot of time giving you an understanding of money and the nitty gritty of our property investment formula, along with some of the key factors that affect property prices and investment in this country.

Now it's time to take all that knowledge a step further in what we call the Buyer's Decision Quadrant. Comprising four key components, the quadrant sets out a framework for the decisions that we typically make when we buy property. These are: price, location, land proportion and quality of dwelling (see Figure 15 overleaf). It takes into account all of the property analysis we discussed in Chapter 6 and presents it in a neat quadrant ready for you to apply to your own investment property process.

There's a fair chance that you already factor in some or all of these components when you're in the market looking to invest, but by creating a framework we'll show you what aspects can be compromised and what are non-negotiable. This will put you in a much stronger position to make a sound investment.

By following through each section, you'll also eliminate the emotional factor and other elements that can derail an otherwise strong investment. Many of us just don't have the ability to compromise on certain things when it comes to property, but the quadrant gives you an objective, unbiased framework to reference so you can cut to the chase!

It's also worth mentioning that we ourselves use the quadrant every single time we approach a property. We call it the science of property investment. Once you have a handle on it, and can work through each of the sections, you'll never look at the property investment process any other way.

Figure 15: The Buyer's Decision Quadrant

Price   Location

Dwelling Quality   Land Content

 Location

You should know now (hopefully!) that for us, location is key and that is why we always put location as the first and most important component of the buyer's decision quadrant. As we've discussed previously, most of us head straight to the 'looking' part of the process first – you only need to jump online to the key property websites to see that 'area' is often the first selection criteria to enter.

Quite simply, the location does 80 per cent of the heavy lifting, so for us it's one of the non-negotiables in our buyer's decision quadrant. In other words, 80 per cent of your return will be derived from the area in which you buy, so location is king from a return-on-investment point of view. Don't be like the vast majority of investors who choose property type first and suburb second; it should definitely be the suburb first and then buy the best property you can comfortably afford in that suburb.

While location is the first consideration, it's also the hardest to get right. This is because you need to assess 'true demand' which means working out the areas that are sought-after for the right reasons. A lot of the time this is tricky because you might not have enough of an understanding of the property market in different areas. This is especially true when investing interstate. The key things we look at to establish 'true demand' are what does the area offer residents in terms of lifestyle and employment – the opportunity to earn income?

Now the interesting aspect to location when it comes to investing is that we're really riding on the coat-tails of the owner occupier. As we mentioned earlier, they've already done the hard work in creating demand for the areas they want to live in, by paying sustained emotional values for those properties. Now it's our job as investors to capitalise on that by swooping in and buying the assets that we know will be sought-after by the marketplace.

BRYCE's Location Tip

Another interesting tip for choosing a location is to look for 'gentrification'. This is where wealthier people are moving into a specific area that was once run-down and often 'blue collar'. If you can do your research and buy in such an area, there's great money to be made. Today, there are many examples of gentrified suburbs across Australia (and the world), but what are the signs you can look out for that indicate that this process is starting?

• It must be close to the city or beach and be deemed attractive by those with more money

• The main shopping strip should have very few 'for lease' or 'for sale' signs

• Is there a creative class or culture – where architects and designers are looking to flex their creative muscle?

• Look for areas where people are willing to move into homes to renovate

• The location needs to have historic homes – built before World War II – in pockets close to the CBD

• There must be a high proportion of owner-occupiers who are house-proud

• Public and private money should be being spent – look for state, federal or local government investment in the area

• Take the time to walk around and observe the suburb. You can pick up the sounds and smells that indicate the type of people living there

• Look at the demographics on the ABS website: find out if incomes are rising above the state national average; or whether the number of professionals in the area is above the average and rising.

Price

If the location is usually the first thing buyers look at, then the cost or price of the property is next, and it's typically the most inflexible aspect of the quadrant. If you've followed the Five Essential Steps to start in Part One, and the Four Pillars – A, B, C and D – of the property investment formula, you'll already have a pretty firm idea of your borrowing power, as well as what you can afford according to the area you're after.

The budget is an important factor to consider – especially as investors – and there are two key questions you'll need to answer in order to satisfy this part of the framework:

→ What does your household believe it can afford to buy today?

→ How will you sustain that asset over time?

You need to remember that at its heart, property has significant costs to get into and these are even more significant when you want to get out. Before you embark on an investment journey, you need to be truly honest with yourself and your family about whether you can actually afford the property today and afford to hold it over the long term.

In our experience, a single property investment could cost you up to an extra 20 per cent in a year if you have to divest from it, so it pays to do the maths and sound research first. In many cases, people jump straight into buying property because their mates around the barbecue are all doing it and suddenly everyone's an expert. However, it is a big decision and if you can get it right from the start, i.e. it's within your budget – you'll be in a much stronger position to hold that asset for the long term.

BEN's Cost Tip

Look at your budget carefully, using the tools we've provided throughout this book. Also, factor in a buffer for things like interest rate movements (which most likely won't stay as low as they are at time of writing), as well as the cash flow changes over the next few years that are going to put pressure on your household spending. Effectively you want to stress test your household to work out what you can comfortably afford.

 ## Land content

You need to think about land proportion as property type. Whether you opt for house and land 20 km out of the city, a mid-rise development or a single-dwelling property, the important question to ask yourself is what your money will buy you within a desirable location. As well as how much land you can afford in that location.

There are many types of property assets across Australia. Not only do you have to consider the condition of particular properties, which we cover next, but you need to look at the types of properties available that you can afford in that area. In short, the more land and house you get the better the return prospects but that all depends on how much you've got to spend. The important thing to note here is to buy the best property you can comfortably afford in the highest land value area. If you can afford a house then great, but if you can only afford a townhouse or an apartment then don't see this as the booby prize. See it as a great opportunity to stay in the location and buy the best investment-grade property you can get your hands on.

You also need to think about whether that property will suit an owner-occupier's needs. If you correctly locate properties with high owner-occupier appeal in an area of high interest for that type of property – and you get in there before everyone else discovers it – you have found pure property gold!

As we mentioned under the cost quadrant, property is not cheap. A poor selection decision might have you thinking there will be higher interest in a property that has an extra 500 m² of backyard space for the kids, but is located an extra 10 km out from the city and all the 'action'. This could potentially cost you big time when it comes to capital growth returns. So it pays to be smart, to do your due diligence by working through the quadrant and organise your thoughts to think ahead to what the market place is looking for.

Dwelling quality

Is the property the owner-occupier is considering shiny and new, appealing to the elevated status you want to achieve, or is it dated and fusty – the perfect 'ripe for renovation' property that you can live in short term but has the option to upgrade in time?

Without wriggle room on the cost, and if you are satisfied with the location, it's often this quadrant that can be the easiest to compromise on. You might opt for an older dwelling that's a little cheaper but bigger than something newer or of better quality.

Quality of dwelling is all about the implied 'status' of the property – just as there is implied status to a suburb – and what condition the property is in. Here are some of the key factors to consider:

→ In what year was the property built?

→ Does it show signs of wear and tear that you can see?

→ What is the quality like? Does it have buyer appeal?

→ What would people think if you bought it?

Again, this is another area that can be compromised if you can't compromise on price and aren't willing to compromise on location. At the end of the day, you must consider the bling or fatigue factor in the context of whether that purchase will make a good investment. You do this by tapping into the headspace of emotional buyers. As we've discussed before, we generally prefer old and established over new and shiny, because of the superior proven return potential.

BRYCE's Case Study

Consider a family of four with two young kids looking to buy a new owner-occupier property. They've got their budget sorted, they have decided on their desirable location, but they realise they may not be able to get the size of property they want because they prefer to buy in such a desirable location. For this family, their decision has to be compromised. Due to the family's size, they will most likely not be looking for a one-bedroom or even two-bedroom apartment, so that cuts out some of the options. But would they opt for a three-bedroom townhouse or a three-bedroom single dwelling with a small courtyard, so long as there is a park nearby where the kids can play? It's these decisions we as property investors are trying to tap into because they are questions faced by property buyers all over the world. Ultimately, this family can't move on size and budget – hence this is the most fixed component of the quadrant. They might then compromise on location, or compromise on the dwelling size by opting for a townhouse in their preferred area. Location means more to them than the property. For others, it might be the other way around; the property land and size might mean more to them. This is what makes property investing so challenging yet so exciting, solving this puzzle to get the best returns!

BRYCE's Tip

As a professional investor, I look at hundreds of properties every month and physically walk through many of them. Once I hone in on something I like, I'll back-test its performance to see how many times it's been sold and what the compounding growth rate has been. So here's an observation I've made after doing this exercise hundreds of times: 1970s apartments consistently outperform 1990s apartments. Why? We think it's because they're well built, with less expensive amenities and consequently lower owners' corporation fees. This makes them more appealing to owner-occupiers as well as investors. The beauty of these 1970s' apartments is that they are typically more affordable too. You're better off buying the 'ugly duckling' because in another 20, 30 or 40 years, both those '70s and '90s apartments will be considered 'old'. But be smart – don't go in blind – have a plan, use the quadrant and compare apples with apples.

PART TWO WRAP-UP

You've now learned the foundations of investing in Part One, the science and theory of investing in Part Two, so you're ready to build an understanding about the strategies we use with our clients every day in Part Three. This is the most exciting part of the book where you can bring all of your knowledge to the fore and learn about the practical side of property investing.

To sum up, tapping into the headspace of many owner-occupiers' decision quadrants will give you an edge in better asset selection. This is because you know what's going on in their minds emotionally, relating to price, location, land proportion and quality of dwelling. You've probably already been doing something similar yourself in one way or another, if you've ever bought a home. Remember, 70 per cent of the market is controlled by owner-occupier buyers – emotional buyers. They set the area price and as investors we simply ride on their coat-tails.

By using this framework, you can organise your 'asset selection' thoughts sequentially and not waste your time on factors that are irrelevant. We've developed the quadrant based on our many years' experience in researching tens of thousands of properties. Just as it works for us and our clients in getting outperform results, we're hoping it can work for you too.

Don't go after the investor stock – where the majority of property is owned by investors – it's the wrong way to go. Remember you want to be a price-taker, not a price-maker! In other words, there's no need to re-invent the wheel. As we just mentioned, if you can find out what owner-occupiers want in the locations that you've identified as investment-grade, (because it has high owner-occupier interest), then you can simply ride in the slip stream and take all the benefits.

Of course, it's also worth considering what kind of investor you want to be, because there are a number of different strategies you can adopt. Essentially, it all comes down to whether you want to be an active or passive investor. You need to work this out because your property portfolio success hinges on whether you would rather sit back and watch the rental income come in and the investment value steadily increase (passive), or you'd prefer to get your hands dirty by taking a much more proactive approach (active). With the more proactive approach, you'll be looking to manufacture growth in equity and/or income by adopting value-add strategies to maximise the potential of your portfolio.

This is a great segue into Part Three which is all about strategies. Your future as an investor and the strategies you decide on will largely depend on the kind of investor you want to be. If you have a demanding job it might be more difficult for you to be an active investor because you may not have the time to put into your investment research activities. Conversely, if you have all the time in the world you might become completely swamped with information and get stuck moving forward.

As you read through our strategies, you'll probably pick up on a few phrases that you've heard quoted in the media, such as 'renovator's delight' or 'jewel in the crown'. We take it a step further, showing each strategy and what sort of buyer's risk profile it suits, how you need to prepare your cash flow, your borrowing power, and whether the strategy is easy or difficult – and why.

So if you're ready to get active, read on!

Summary so far...

✓ Buyers Decision Quadrant

✓ Property Market Mechanism

✓ Building your Team

✓ The Property Investment Formula

✓ Investment Foundations

✓ Industry Players

✓ Money SMARTS

✓ The Five Essential Steps

✓ The Four Foundation Levers

✓ Money Mindset

✓ Personal Values and Goals

PART THREE

ACTION

"Success is nothing more than a few
simple disciplines, practised every day."

—JIM ROHN

AS PART of our enjoyment of knowledge-sharing, we've worked with some of the country's top publishers and editors, connecting with readers all around Australia. Along the way, we've landed magazine covers and feature stories as well as appeared on various television channels as expert commentators and presented as keynote speakers at property expos and conferences.

By far, we've found that the biggest response from our audience comes when we provide practical, tangible examples that can be actioned. A lot of the property books on the shelves – you may already own a few – don't go far enough into the gold that has made their authors wealthy, or they gloss over the real science behind investing without offering any concrete examples that you can relate to. We've attempted to cover off all of this in the first two parts, while adhering to our philosophy that property investing is a process, not an event, and that it's not a one-size-fits-all proposition.

As we move into this last part of the book, we want to share with you the fruits of our labour over the past two decades, because we know that with the right information and approach, you can achieve property success, just as we have within our own lives and the lives of our clients.

We've broken up this part into three distinct sections to make it easier to digest. The first section is what's important to know when it comes to your own personal investment profile and how that will help you when you're building your portfolio. The second section covers the actual strategies we have identified over our experience in the industry. We break down why they work and offer handy tips and tricks to watch out for.

Finally, we present what you've all been waiting for – the actual proof of how to earn a $2,000 weekly passive income. We do this by presenting you with six scenarios and, in a similar vein, break them down so that you can see how they work, where the wealth is created and importantly, how you can do it yourself.

Once you have worked through the previous parts of the book and unpacked your cash flow, you'll be in a much better place to strategically choose your property investment pathway. Think of it as one of those children's 'Choose your own adventure' books where there is a multitude of possible endings. You want to ensure your ending is going to generate the best possible outcome, rather than finish up in a different spot and wonder what the heck happened.

At the moment, the property investment industry is currently an unregulated sector, which means that there are a number of 'cowboys' offering their views, options and advice on what they think is best. Remember to ask yourself if they are advising or selling you a one-size-fits-all concept. Don't be lured by their slick presentations or shiny brochures. You'll see them in the newspapers or spruiking their agendas using cheap television advertisements or radio spots. They come in a variety of forms including sales agents, property marketers and fringe practitioners, such as mortgage brokers and accountants. Our particular favourite is the promise of tens of thousands of dollars in instant equity – so beware!

First let's give you an insight into the ins and outs of how to create your risk assessment and get to understand what you want from investing. This will ultimately help you to better understand the most relevant strategy to adopt and enable you to create wealth in the short or long term.

LEARNING ABOUT YOU | 8

You've made the decision to join the many Australians who enjoy property investing as their preferred vehicle to reach their financial goals. Next up, you need to work out two key components:

1. **Investor considerations** – relating to your ability, desire, skill and experience as an investor

2. **Tactical considerations** – the variables which make up part of the implementation process. These include research requirements, cash flow position and investment outcomes.

We touched on this at the end of the last chapter but it's important that you work through these areas before you jump into the market because successful property investment (specifically investing that's going to set you up for life) is a long-term prospect, and you need to be on the right page from the start.

Investor considerations

What are your levels of knowledge, experience and qualifications?

Here's a universal truth about human nature: people will choose the 'line of least resistance'. But as with anything in life, the more you put in the more you get out. It's the same for property investment. What about your experience? It's important to self-assess to understand your own level of expertise, which could help you avoid mistakes down the track. Do you have any formal and relevant qualifications? These can be a huge benefit to you as you start your investment journey. By qualifications, we mean things like being a licensed builder, an interior designer or architect. The more sophisticated strategies can also benefit from other types of credentials, such as being an accountant or conveyancer, because they can potentially influence the types of strategies you choose.

What is your level of risk?

Any adviser who is doing their job properly will work through a risk assessment profile with you, which outlines the level of risk you are willing to take on. Pretty much everything in life carries some form of risk and in the case of property investing each strategy will contain more or less risk than the next. We generally rank risk in the following order:

→ High risk

→ Moderate to high risk

→ Moderate risk

→ Low to moderate risk

→ Low risk.

It's critical to establish your own level of risk that you feel personally comfortable with. No one can make this decision for you but it will affect the strategies available to you, so it pays to think long and hard about this from the start. In our view, most property investing is low risk if you are buying for the long term and in proven locations. Some property investing can be medium to high risk, for example investing in mining towns. When you assess your own risk tolerance, you need to think in terms of general investment risk plus the risk associated with using debt (as leverage risk) and general property risk in terms of location, type and condition. High levels of debt will increase your risk, so you need to be 100 per cent comfortable about this. That's why detailed cash flow assessments become so critical in the wealth-building process.

How much time have you got to spend?

The luxury of time! It's that most sought-after quality and we always want more of it. If you don't have enough time to allocate to your strategy and to implement it, it'll simply slip into the realm of nothingness or you'll need to outsource it to a professional. If you are in a position to dedicate time to your portfolio outside of your work commitments, you'll be more likely to succeed.

What sort of investor do you want to be?

Following on from how much time you've got is the type of investor you want to be. We have a simple measure for you to work out how much of an investor you are. Basically, it comes down to the time you've got to allocate to your investment activity: the more time you allocate, the less you're an investor. You're likely to be one of the following:

→ **Active worker.** You're hands-on and 100 per cent, full-time committed to property investing through your own property developing.

→ **Active weekend worker.** You're not full time, but you spend evenings and weekends renovating your investment properties from time to time.

→ **Active manager.** You're an active project manager; spending plenty of your leisure time on property matters. It's like a second job, so you'll need to be prepared for that.

→ **Passive investor.** You're a 'true' investor, meaning you buy and hold your investment. You don't want to give any full-time or even heavy time commitment to investing. You might even outsource the process to professionals, realising you lack all the skills required to do it on your own. You'll still track the returns and remain interested but you're not 'hands-on'.

→ **Pure investor.** You're so time-poor, earning a great income with what you do so well, that you entrust everything to other professionals. You pay their fees and get your return reports each year.

Establishing what sort of investor you want to be from the outset will help you decide the level of involvement you want to have. It may also give you the head space required to make it work in the long term.

How long do you want to be in the market?

From a property investment perspective, we usually assess this against the following timetable:

→ **Speculator:** 0 to 6 years (not an investor at all – a gambler in our eyes)

→ **Short term:** 7 to 15 years

→ **Medium term:** 16 to 25 years

→ **Long term:** ideally indefinite, but any period greater than 25 years.

It's important to assess this because the entry, holding and potential exit costs of property can be very high. If your property is investment-grade, we would advise you to hold on to it for as long as possible. We are big fans of holding property indefinitely, which allows you to enjoy the great levels of passive income. It also means you're in a position to pass on your estate to future family generations, leaving a legacy (although sometimes we do advise against this).

What's your current wealth position?

If you know what you've got to play with, you're much more likely to formulate the right strategy. While we will generally recommend a conservative approach, if you already have a large cash base and a property portfolio, you might be more willing to take a more aggressive position. That is all up for assessment.

Tactical considerations

How much time do you need to spend on area/location research?

Finding an investment-grade property takes time because you need to combine a level of research with gaining some property invest-ment knowledge that also fits in with the strategy you choose. As a general rule, the following is the recommended time to dedicate to area and location research:

→ **Basic:** 50 hours

→ **Standard:** 200 hours

→ **Advanced:** 500 hours (Yep – to be a master you need to put the hours in).

Why so many hours? Well, your challenge here is to start with 15,000 suburbs and drill down to ultimately picking one! It's not an easy exercise. In fact, in our business we have full-time researchers whose job it is to drill down to just a handful of suburbs where we can locate properties before they become popular with other investors. Try looking at it this way; if you can dedicate four hours a night for two weeks, you'll be at a basic level in no time! Extend that out and in just under two months you will be well on your way to being very well researched. Trust me, the armchair ride gets easier once you have implemented the plan, we promise! Or you can also outsource some of the work to a professional.

BRYCE's Tip

Remember! Effective searching is not just about logging onto real estate websites and sipping on a latte flicking through properties and areas. Start from the 'macro' at state and city level, and then move onto 'micro' – suburb, localised neighbourhood, street and finally property.

How much time do you need to spend on property research?

Again, once you've identified the area or location, you'll need to spend more time considering individual property requirements. You can broaden this out to the population of the area, localised neighbourhood and street appeal, and then get into the nitty gritty of the property itself, such as size, bedrooms, living areas, floor plan and homeliness, etc. This is what we recommend:

→ **Basic:** 10 hours

→ **Standard:** 20 hours

→ **Advanced:** 50 hours

Remember! It's important to know that spending more than 50 hours will most likely deliver an investment-grade property that should perform beautifully. But this won't guarantee a bargain, as many top-performing properties are never sold at bargain prices.

What's my cash flow and borrowing power – what price point can I buy for?

If you've worked through Parts One and Two of this book, you'll already know your cash flow and borrowing positions. Understanding where you're at financially will enable you to make sound decisions about what price point to buy at, rather than a decision that could have a devastating effect on your family. You also need to ensure you can meet all loan repayments and have contingency funds in case you're set back for whatever reason. We always provide realistic purchase price ranges like with your income, as well as take into account surplus cash flows whenever we help clients with their plans.

When's the right time to buy?

This one's a darling of the media. Any day of the week you'll find a property story in the business section detailing the debate about when you buy. It's a great grab and it always sells papers. The reality is that all properties require different approaches and that comes down to the strategy you choose. Don't listen to the media – listen to your adviser!

With more and more property data and greater analytics tools now available, the science of timing the market is getting better and better as each year goes by. Timing your entry into the market is important because you don't want to buy in at the top of the market and spend the next five years waiting for the next growth cycle. The goal is to time your purchase maybe 12 to 18 months before the market really kicks in. Then you get the benefit of buying close to the bottom without too much competition for the best property assets in that market.

What about the tax implications?

While we're not tax agents and don't purport to be tax experts, we suggest you engage someone who is to sit on your team. Make sure they're professional and qualified so that they can explain the tax outcomes of any strategy you adopt. In our strategies, we refer to your taxation position in the following ways:

→ **Negative gearing.** The cost of holding the investment property is higher than the income at the time of purchase, resulting in a potential loss and possible tax refund.

→ **Neutral gearing.** The income (rent) and the outgoings are pretty much on par at the time of purchase, resulting in a neutral tax outcome.

→ **Positive gearing.** The income (rent) on the property is more than any costs (e.g. interest and maintenance costs, etc.) at the time of purchase.

18 INVESTMENT STRATEGIES

9

Now with an understanding of where you sit as an investor and what you need to invest to become one, it's time to introduce you to our strategies. We've created 18 specific strategies that we believe cover off all the mainstream reasons why you're looking to invest in property. These are tried and tested by us and we use and refer to these by name every day as we work with our clients. The strategies take into account all of the investor and tactical considerations from Chapter 8, to make it easier to compare and understand. Remember though that property should only require 10 hours per property per year to maintain if you are a passive investor – so once you've put in the hard yards using our strategies, hopefully you'll be able to sit back and reap the benefits of your work. It's worth mentioning here again that although your search for investment-grade property may take many, many hours, the actual time required for managing each property should only be about 10 hours per year. Seems worth it, doesn't it?

In our experience, property investing is a study of two parts: the economy and human nature (human interest and human behaviour). We're especially interested in the way these two relate to each other from a return-on-investment perspective, because it's by studying people and why they want to live in an area that we get an understanding of demand, which ultimately allows a property to hold its value, and gives you, the investor, a stronger return.

Our 18 strategies each fit into one of these four categories:

→ Area strategies for capital growth

→ Property selection strategies for capital growth

→ Area strategies for yield/income

→ Property strategies for yield/income

Each of these can be read as a powerful standalone strategy, but they can also be interlinked and intertwined depending on which pathway you choose. Remember that we are very big on creating tailor-made solutions for our clients, so what's right for one person might not be the best fit for someone else.

With all of that in mind, let's get into the strategies!

Area strategies for capital growth

STRATEGY 1 –
The Proven Performer

The Proven Performer offers a reliable and regular performance, featuring a property location with very consistent longer-term capital growth over an extended period of time – say 30 years. Proven Performers typically offer strong income growth. These locations are usually fully developed with tight planning guidelines and are in high demand. They offer great lifestyle and the properties in these locations are often character or period homes (think suburbs like South Yarra in Melbourne, Mosman in Sydney, Bulimba in Brisbane).

Investors it's suited to?

Passive or Pure investors are attracted to these areas. You'll need a solid cash flow as well as higher borrowings because of the better than average capital growth prospects.

Difficulty level?

Low to Moderate. These are your blue-chip areas which are not hard to find but the challenge is picking the right investment-grade property at the right time and the right price. You'll just need to do a bit of research to locate the better streets and housing stock. And when you do you'll have a strong investment horizon with good rental appeal too.

→ **Area research:** Basic. Focus on quality pockets within the broader location

→ **Property research:** Basic to standard.

Risk and time allocation level?

Lower risk. The only risk involved might be how much debt you're prepared to take on as these properties are generally priced on the high side. The pressure point here is selecting the asset and beating the competition, while understanding the right value in today's market.

Price point?

From $350,000 upwards in some major cities for entry-level units, but it's unlikely you'll secure anything under $500,000, so this is usually your starting point. Keep purchases under $1.2 million for houses. (In regional areas the prices will be lower – and yes they do exist, just on a smaller scale.)

Tax implications and when to buy?

These properties are negatively geared to start, with positive returns within 8 to 12 years and they provide a strong income in retirement. This strategy is a set and forget – buy/hold.

STRATEGY 2 – Rare Earth

Rare Earth is about investing in and understanding land and its relation to appreciating values and scarcity. We're not interested in acquiring vacant land here, but more land with an income-producing dwelling that is of a sound investment-grade dwelling. Think waterfront homes or dwellings with excellent access and location.

Investors it's suited to?

Passive or Pure investors. You'll need solid surplus cash flows because the initial shortfall between income and the cost of holding the asset will have an impact, until your investment grows in value and the rental returns grow over time.

Difficulty level?

Low. You need to know the amount of vacant land, rezoned land or backfill land to understand its scarcity within an area. From a Rare Earth strategy perspective, there shouldn't be any real vacant land. These locations have a very strong upside when they have a run in value growth, and rare earth locations have a significant capital growth story. Many investors won't sell these for that very good reason – location, location, location!

Risk and time allocation level?

Low. These areas aren't so hard to understand or find, but you'll need to allocate time and effort if you're talking about large city locations, because when they come up they get snapped up quickly.

Price point?

Apartment entry level is upwards of $500,000. Most properties sit in the $750,000 to $1,500,000 range, with some up to $2 million. (In regional areas the prices will be lower – and yes once again they do exist as good sized regional towns do have upmarket pockets too.)

Tax implications and when to buy?

These properties are negatively geared, with good taxation outcomes for high-income households. Get in and lock in for the great journey ahead, the capital growth and actual dollar returns in these locations are simply wonderful if you can afford them.

STRATEGY 3 – Million Dollar Strip

These suburbs come under the 'if I had unlimited money I'd live here' category. These prize-winning addresses leverage off very high 'status and bragging' appeal, great 'dress circle' neighbourhood appeal and wonderful street appeal, such as tree-lined streets, beachfront boulevard, etc.

Investors it's suited to?

Passive or Pure investors. This strategy requires high incomes and large amounts of surplus cash flow out of the household's budget, as well as solid borrowing power.

Difficulty level?

It's not hard to work out where these areas are located, just look for the most expensive real estate within a location. The investment gold is more towards the median value levels and these properties leverage off the grand addresses and properties in the area.

Risk and time allocation level?

Traditionally low risk and very predictable performers. We wouldn't advocate paying the established benchmark pricing (top dollar) in these areas – stick with the median value levels, which ensure less risk. Therefore, your time will be best spent picking the eyes out of this market and understanding where values can go as measured by income growth.

Price point?

From $800,000 for units up to $3 million for houses. Stick to buying the property below median value for the area, this will ensure you get some income (yield) returns early on.

Tax implications and when to buy?

These properties are very negatively geared to start off with, with huge potential for capital growth and sound, high-income earning taxation offsets.

STRATEGY 4 – Changing Places…. Changing Faces

This strategy relates to old, working-class areas as close to CBDs as possible. They are the areas that have been (or are about to be) transformed into hip and happening, urban renewal locations. The term is 'gentrified' and because they are more affordable for younger people they are becoming popular. Areas such as Collingwood or Richmond in Melbourne and Alexandria or Macdonaldtown in Sydney are good examples of fully-gentrified suburbs.

Investors it's suited to?

Passive or Pure investors, as well as an Active Manager type investor in the future. This strategy still requires you to put your hand in your pocket, as you will be paying more for property here than you would be for a bigger house out in the 'burbs, but the future prospects of good growth will justify the spend.

Difficulty level?

This strategy requires lots of research and an 'investor grade eye'. If you're not willing to build your knowledge about this one, you should look to outsource the research. Most of these properties require some updating, so if you can handle that you'll be winning.

Risk and time allocation level?

Low to Moderate risk. The challenge for these areas is for every five you get right, there is potentially one area that could take longer to gentrify. The short-term risk of losing capital value is very low if you've researched the area adequately, but again the upside is well worth the effort.

Price point?

From as low as $350,000 for units to $1,000,000 for houses around Australia. (Again they can exist in our largest, older, regional towns, but forget units, just focus on houses upwards from $350,000 close by the really wealthy suburbs.)

Tax implications and when to buy?

These properties are negatively geared to start off with, but if strong growth is experienced this could result in the strategy delivering a potential neutral and positive position quicker than might be expected. If the area is selected right and the purchase is timed well, there's potential in the short term that the investment will outperform in the form of strong capital growth. Add this to the attractive price point and you can see why we love this strategy, even with its degree of difficulty!

STRATEGY 5 – The City Fling

The City Fling is all about pure lifestyle locations loaded with amenities for young people, such as running tracks, cafes, gyms, the beach, music and clubs. These are inner-city locations with residents who are well educated and have strong disposable incomes for their age. There are good tenant options, but there's also demand for those seeking to get into the market too. This creates an underlying demand in these areas which results in the strong capital growth they deliver. But one important point – this strategy is NOT the actual city itself – it's the fringe. Why? Because actual city property can have mass supply increases very easily, so we avoid it and also avoid the medium- and high-density suburbs in general.

Investors it's suited to?

Passive or Pure investors. This is due to the relative predictability of these areas, with the potential to become more active by seeking out an Ugly Duckling or Renovator's Mission property strategy (more on that later). These areas offer better than average yields because of their popularity with renters who want to live in the 'happening' zone. They also provide good prospects for growth. Borrowing power and reasonable household income surpluses go hand in hand with this area strategy. Most middle class investors can handle this one.

Difficulty level?

It's usually pretty easy to work out these locations – they have good live music or great summer beachside appeal (and are still close to the main city). They're not suburbs with big homes, but more medium density with a high population per square metre of total suburb land area. Classic areas that come to mind are: Bondi, Kings Cross and Manly in Sydney; St Kilda and Prahran in Melbourne; Fortitude Valley and West End in Brisbane; and Subiaco or Northbridge in Perth.

Risk and time allocation level?

Low to Moderate risk with fantastic long-term return potential. The only barriers are sometimes price point and when there is a building boom on, periods of potential oversupply could be created. This strategy still requires some time researching the underlying population and supply forecasts within the location.

Price point?

Ranging from $400,000 for units and starting from $700,000 for townhouses and villas and $900,000 for houses.

Tax implications and when to buy?

These properties are slightly to moderately negatively geared, and if the area performs well they will move to a neutral then to a positive outcome in under 10 years. Your best bet will be to time your move if you can comfortably afford the initial shortfall between the rental income and the debt position.

STRATEGY 6 – The Wave Rider

The Wave Rider is about identifying areas and locations benefiting from the successes of neighbouring locations and suburbs. It suggests that demand for certain accommodation – usually houses

– is exceeding buyers' interest, based on the buyer's decision quadrant we talked about earlier. These buyers will soon turn to the next neighbourhood to still enjoy the best of the amenities the area has to offer. Therefore, these are second-tier locations and when the wave effect of capital growth occurs, one day they too will become blue chip locations.

Investors it's suited to?

Passive or Pure investors. But this strategy can also offer opportunities for the more active style investors. Initial yields are usually better in these locations because the capital growth isn't as consistent but there will potentially be better gains in the future as more people become interested in the location due to affordability pressures. As such, the impact on the household cash flow is not as great compared to buying in premium locations. So from a borrowing power perspective it's more achievable for most investor households.

Difficulty level?

It takes some skill to figure out which locations are likely to become Wave Riders. Focus on watching the demand drivers and supply, distance to amenities, and commute time to employment centres. A novice can easily have a crack at this one but there are risks, so you'll need to be careful. One tip is not to stray too far from train transport in our major cities, and look for the potential for improved local amenities in the immediate area, even when what attracted the owner occupier were the great amenities close by.

Risk and time allocation level?

Moderate risk if you do your homework. High risk if you cut corners, because it relies on choosing an area riding on the success of another. The area research is going to be time-consuming because there are more areas that offer 'fools gold' instead of potential real gold.

Price point?

Units start from $300,000 upwards, and for houses you're looking at $500,000 – higher in Sydney and Melbourne. This strategy also works in our regional markets, but focus on regional cities with populations over 50,000+, with the price point for houses starting around the $200,000 mark. Generally speaking, we don't use this strategy for units.

Tax implications and when to buy?

These properties offer a higher initial yield than their blue-chip neighbours, but they are still slightly negatively geared, depending on the interest rate of the day. They are likely to become positively geared in five to seven years if you time the market right. Most households can usually afford this strategy and are able to borrow to make it happen.

Summary of area growth strategies	
Proven Performer	Rare Earth
Million Dollar Strip	Changing Places
City Fling	Wave Rider

Property selection strategies for capital growth

STRATEGY 7 – Scarce Diamond

Astute investors understand the Scarce Diamond very well. It's when the actual dwelling itself has strong owner-occupier appeal, with character and period charm usually the order of the day. Crucially, these properties do their own capital growth lifting, just like a vintage car, rare coin or stamp that rises in value over time due to its scarcity and mainstream appeal. High demand means these beauties outperform in value growth return.

Investors it's suited to?

Passive or Pure investors, with potential for Active Investors to add value. Some diamonds need to be 'polished'! A moderate or above average cash flow is needed.

Difficulty level?

Here, you need to grasp the difference between things that age gracefully and offer timeless attraction versus those that don't. You don't have to look too far to gauge this – it's usually the mainstream opinion and belief, so if you can tap into that, you'll be well served. Just don't make a mistake and get drawn to 'flashier' property stock that will date poorly.

Risk and time allocation level?

Low risk if bought at market value. Some buyers buy these at a premium rather than the current market value, so make sure you don't lose your head and pay an emotional price for this type of asset. Finding them isn't rocket science, but you might need to broaden your search as these properties are usually tightly held. If you add up the time to understand the real value of the property plus doing your research, only to be gazumped at auction time and time again, you begin to see how it can take a fair amount of effort and time to finally lock down a property.

Price point?

From $200,000 right up to $5 million, the difference being that those in the $200,000 location could represent upper quartile ranges of full values within that regional market. The same applies to the $5 million properties too!

Tax implications and when to buy?

These properties are negatively geared at the start, but with good rental income potential at the lower price points, as renters want to show them off too. We'd expect them to become neutrally geared and then positively geared in 8 to 12 years. You might have to adopt a 'seize the day' philosophy for these properties – as when they come up they are snapped up very quickly!

STRATEGY 8 – Ugly Duckling

This one's an equity play with an active strategy, where you find a property with 'good bones' and in due course renovate or restore it, (but it can be livable in the meantime). At some point you will bring it to market to realise even further wealth gains. The trick is in the buying so you can derive further profit out of your efforts. You'll need to factor in any cash flow and borrowing buffers you believe might be required, plus more to cover for the shortfall in rental income during the renovation period. It's usually the short-term, quick cosmetic equity gain harvest that makes this strategy so rewarding, because the gain can be turned into a further equity release to potentially buy another property, giving you a multiplier of wealth effect. When you're doing your calculations about how much to borrow it's best to be conservative. Before making cosmetic renovations, you will get a lower rent due to the tiredness of the property, but post reno you should get a good rental boost. A minimum rule of thumb is for every dollar you spend on your cosmetic reno, you need to get two dollars back in the final valuation post renovation.

Investors it's suited to?

Active Worker, Active Weekender or Active Manager.

Difficulty level?

Knowledge is an important ingredient in this play. You need to focus on what the end sales value should be and make sure that you're within a budget delivering adequate returns. If you want to save money, it comes down to labour so if you're good with your hands or have a trade, all the better. Time and project management skills are a must, otherwise your effort to achieve a quick gain will be lost.

Risk and time allocation level?

Moderate, but the bigger the project the higher the risk. This one's for those with high energy and a strong work ethic! It will be very time-consuming, so you'll want to be sure you're happy that this will become a second job for a period of time. Factor into your costings some blowouts. This will ensure your project will have the right margin in it to be worthwhile.

Price point?

As this strategy is based around buying a tired property and bringing it up to current market appeal, it can work in any price range. It's about buying under market value when you compare the property to other similar stock on offer and then realising its potential to add value.

Tax implications and when to buy?

There are great potential tax benefits because you're renovating. Some will be immediate and others depreciable over time. It doesn't really matter when you buy because it can work in any market cycle. If you do the project well, it will stack up. And remember, you can also buy the Ugly Duckling, rent it out for a few years and then turn it into the black swan you know it can be.

STRATEGY 9 – The Shoulder Rider

This one's all about focusing on a unit purchase in the best location possible for the dollar outlay. We've talked about this in earlier parts of the book, and it's a strategy for buying existing older style units in a small block, rather than new property, and enjoying the ride! So focus on getting the area right first, somewhere with a number of apartments due to come on line at a significantly higher price point, and then buy the older-style apartment in that area.

You'll get it at a discount to the new flashy apartment but benefit from the artificially inflated median price once the new stock receives its certificate of occupancy. Over a period of time, the new flashy property will be just like yours. Your older-style property will return a greater percentage in capital growth while also returning slightly better yields.

Investors it's suited to?

Suits all five of our investor types. This is because units and apartments present as good 'shells' and in a lot of cases are very rentable in their current state for a long period of time. However, all investors can be involved in the non-structural renovation, which should still keep the total cost under that of buying the flashy, new off-the-plan property or you shouldn't have bought it. Moderate cash flow is needed with the lending range determined by the amount of surplus income and rental income you can get.

Difficulty level?

You'll need to study the area to work out how many new apartments are coming on line, as well as understand how off-the-plan projects are costed and priced. (To cost an off-the-plan apartment is easy and it's the same for houses – simply divide the selling price by the internal living area to work out a per-square-metre cost.) In the right locations you want to aim for off-the-plan properties to set new price point records for that location – that's how you shoulder ride!

Risk and time allocation level?

Low to Moderate. You'll be cushioned by the higher unit price point and won't have too much market turndown risk. If you put the time into researching, it's well worth the effort.

Price point?

Baseline around most capital cities from $350,000 and higher for

Sydney ($600,000) and Melbourne ($500,000). A good rule of thumb is to buy this property in the price range no lower than 25 per cent less and no higher than the current median price – pre the arrival of the new apartment stock. So if the median value is $500,000 for the suburb, buy within the $375,000 to $500,000 range.

Tax implications and when to buy?

Properties are negatively geared, moving to neutrally geared in six to ten years as a general rule and depending on the price point. It's a great strategy when you time the market, but don't commit until you know the project has the necessary pre-sales to move forward to completion. You don't want to buy a bargain and then find out the new development isn't going ahead.

STRATEGY 10 –
Renovator's Mission

The Renovator's Mission strategy is a hands-on approach, whereby you make structural changes in an effort to improve an existing dwelling and bring it up to a standard comparable to that of the majority of properties in that neighbourhood. It's really about making old new again! Your focus is on maximising the potential equity gain here, which we call equity harvesting.

Investors it's suited to?

Active. It really doesn't get any more hands-on than this. You need time, energy, planning and a budget to get this one happening. It will be a full-time job or at the very least feel like a full-time second job. So make sure you are up for it and factor in an appropriate wage for yourself/selves into your budget as well as buffers. Allow for about a 25 per cent overrun on cost and cash. Therefore, your borrowing power needs to be quite high and you need some equity or cash savings behind you, which will increase the risk.

Difficulty level?

Renovator's Mission is certainly not for everyone. There are many who have come before you and failed miserably, so you want to make sure you have a solid to significant wealth base first. It's not for novices, although it is often promoted to mums and dads. Having trade contacts to keep costs down will help, so we reckon this is best suited to those who have knowledge around building.

- **Area research:** Look for areas with liveability and lifestyle appeal, which will serve you well in the long run.
- **Property research:** Be careful not to overcapitalise on the asset. Keep within 25 per cent of the median value for like properties within the location.

Risk and time allocation level?

High risk – high reward! But buying a property with 'potential' market value does provide some comfort. Forget any real free time too – this one will take up all of it!

Price point?

The lower 25 to 50 per cent median value quartile in that location. This strategy can work in many locations around Australia.

Tax implications and when to buy?

Properties are negatively geared, and will often move to neutral or positive with the completion of the works. If the property isn't rented, the renovations you undertake might not be immediately deductible. We'd recommend seeing a good tax accountant to help you with these costs and tax matters. You should be able to buy these properties in all market cycles.

STRATEGY 11 – Reliable and Durable

It might not have the good looks, but it's a solid investment that's stood the test of time, age and internally it is very liveable, if a little worn. These are not renovation projects, but more durable investments in the long run in terms of upkeep and maintenance. Floors and walls are in good condition and so are the kitchens and bathrooms – they are just dated – so these properties have plenty of good years of service ahead of them.

Investors it's suited to?

Passive or Pure investors. The Reliable and Durable could also be renamed 'set and forget' because there should be few unexpected ongoing expenses. These properties are so great from a capital growth perspective because of their initial buy-in price, which makes them a winner in the long term.

Difficulty level?

No high level of knowledge is required to understand this concept, but these properties need strong 'bones' and good floor plans. The soundness of the property's performance will come down to the level of upkeep required to keep it performing well for you, and the property must be in the right suburb! Don't cut corners – make sure you take the time to understand these properties and what you should be paying for them. With any property you buy, it's smart to get a building and pest inspection, but with these properties it's mandatory.

Risk and time allocation level?

Low to Moderate because these properties are usually priced below the median or average for the same property types (units, villas and houses) and their number of bedrooms in that location. You might be lucky and fluke finding one of these properties, but if you put in the extra work you'll benefit in the longer term. Remember, you don't have to live there, so the fact that on first impressions the property is underwhelming shouldn't deter you.

Price point?

This strategy can be applied to every low-, to mid-, to upper-range price point. Naturally it's not going to be at the top-level range because that asset would have been fully renovated and modernised.

Tax implications and when to buy?

Properties start as negatively geared, with above 5 per cent yield even in city locations, which can increase when they become neutrally geared and then eventually positively geared. In regional areas, yield can start around the 6 per cent mark.

STRATEGY 12 – Size Matters

Size Matters focuses on getting as large a block of land or dwelling as possible within the investment criteria that has been set out. Don't be mistaken though – we don't mean buying a large parcel of land just anywhere, like an acre block on the outskirts of town or one of the largest blocks in a new estate, which is often a trap buyers fall into. There is no land scarcity out there, so what we mean is to focus on good land size in a fully developed area. From the actual property standpoint, when we talk size we are usually referring to its number of bedrooms.

Investors it's suited to?

All categories. Your cash flow needs to be reasonable and your borrowing power relative. The right properties in the right location are scarce, and they often come with a price-tag to suit.

Difficulty level?

It's very hard to work out a true measure of land value in established and older areas, so you might need to call on a professional valuer in some instances. It can be hard work due to the fact that these locations and block sizes vary, and even more challenging is that the dwellings influence the overall value. Valuation is made more difficult when some dwellings have been renovated or updated, etc. Therefore, it'll take some time to familiarise yourself with this land value process.

Risk and time allocation level?

Low to Moderate, but increased competition to secure these assets can push the purchase price up, especially if the size of the land makes it a dual dwelling or development site. Competition will be coming from all corners – owner-occupiers looking for that extra land for family and lifestyle, developers and from non-active investors who are smart and see the long-term value in this land. Remember, this has the potential to push the price past its fair market value.

These land opportunities might only come up once or twice a year, so it might be better to try another strategy if this is too long to wait. If it's property size that matters, then you may have more luck securing, say, a large four- or five-bedroom property that sits on an average lot size.

This strategy can be applied to units but we are talking a huge internal size. Some units are two-bedroom but under 50 m^2 (tiny), yet with this strategy a two-bedroom unit will be over 80 m^2 – plus courtyards are a real bonus.

Price point?

Units starting from $500,000 around Australia, again a lot higher in Sydney and Melbourne – anything upwards of $1.2 million. For regional areas, prices are usually from $200,000 upwards. Houses start around $800,000 in capital cities and go up to $1.5 million (and upwards of $3 million in Sydney and Melbourne).

Tax implications and when to buy?

As the size of the dwelling or land size is mainly about capital growth returns rather than yield, this strategy will be negatively geared and move towards a positive income around 10 to 15 years from purchase. As these types of properties are rarer than most, the best time to buy them is when they come up for sale in a city or regional market that is a buyer's market not a seller's market, because there will be reduced competition.

STRATEGY 13 – The Piggy Backer

This strategy is like the Shoulder Rider but it's for houses instead of units. The same principles apply where you buy an older house that will piggy-back off the increase in new stock in that area, that sells for significantly higher prices. It has an extra benefit too: rental yield as a percentage of the property's value will be better than that of their newer counterparts. What we mean by this is that even though the rent you get each week will be lower than for brand new properties, the overall yield percentage is better because your property is lower in value. It's still a capital growth strategy, but higher yields are also in the mix for this strategy.

Investors it's suited to?

Pure or Passive investors. But the door's open to Active Investors who may wish to consider adding value to the house – an ensuite or alfresco area for example – to reflect buyer's demand.

Difficulty level?

You need an in-depth understanding of the thousands of areas that could apply here. It all sounds relatively simple but the level of knowledge needed is significant to ensure you are aware of these types of capital gains. It's usually a long-term strategy but if timed well it could offer the option to capitalise on any equity gains in the short term (three to ten years). Remember we want to locate old property stock – post war or 1960s to '70s houses – where there is a lot of new stock being built close by at significantly higher prices.

Risk and time allocation level?

Low to medium risk if well executed; high if not. This strategy will yield a great return if the future plans for the area materialise, so your timing needs to be right. If you're thinking of going it alone, this strategy could take a lot of time and energy to research the thousands of potential locations.

Price point?

This is 'affordable country' property. Houses from $350,000 upwards in the capital cities and from $200,000 upwards (yes, as low as this) in some regional locations.

Tax implications and when to buy?

Properties are negatively geared initially, or neutral if there are low interest rates for city locations. In regional locations, with low interest rates, they may even be positively geared. Overall, your investment will move to being neutral or positively geared in less than five years, usually as the lower values of the property are offset against good rental income amounts. Timing is critical for this strategy because all of the upside comes down to when the new stock comes onto the market.

Summary of property selection strategies for capital growth	
Diamond	Ugly Duckling
Shoulder Rider	Reno Mission
Reliable and Durable	Size Matters
Piggy-backer	

Area strategies for yield/income

STRATEGY 14 – No Vacancies

No Vacancies is all about finding areas where rental demand is tight, which means vacancy rates are low. These locations can offer higher rental yields due to the underlying demand, as well as some level of growth in values while the demand exists, because many property investors just chase yield or positive cash flow returns and they compete with other buyers. Cities with gross rental yields of 5.5+ per cent combined with vacancy rates of less than 1 to 2 per cent are prime opportunities. Yet at the time of writing, because of the low interest rates of the day, yields are lower as property values across the board have been growing. For regional areas, look for yields higher than 6 per cent and vacancy rates of around 1 per cent.

Investors it's suited to?

Passive or Pure investors. This is about controlling an asset for as little money out of the household budget as possible, which makes it very attractive for everyday Australians. However, we still recommend holding six months of household spending as a cash buffer, just in case.

Difficulty level?

You need to know what makes for an investment-grade property – it's all about the current and future demand for property in that area as well as the stock coming onto the market. Develop your 'eye' and do your research for what the market is looking for, and work out how you're going to beat others to it. Consider diversified employment, population growth, lifestyle qualities, income, the history of the town and future stock.

Risk and time allocation level?

Moderate to low risk, due to the rental demand, lower out-of-pocket cash flow risk and the affordability of the housing stock in question. This game can be time-consuming because very few of the areas you will consider will be investment-grade, and we see this as a medium- to long-term strategy – over 15+ years.

Price point?

Low end of the market: in regional areas you're looking in the $100,000 to $300,000 range (we prefer houses over units). In the city, we're mainly talking about prices below $750,000 for houses and below $500,000 for units, because the really low vacancies only occur in great lifestyle areas where people stay for the long term. You can get really low vacancy rates in other areas – such as mining towns – but due to their boom and bust nature, vacancy rates aren't always low. In fact, they can get shockingly high at the end of a boom mining cycle.

Tax implications and when to buy?

In a low interest rate environment these properties will be more neutrally or positively geared in regional areas and maybe slightly negatively geared in the capital cities. In a regional sense, it's important to get the timing right because these areas traditionally grow in spurts. In the big cities, unless a huge supply of new stock arrives in the area, usually the rental demand is high and vacancy rates are low in the great lifestyle areas.

STRATEGY 15 – The Boomtowners

The Boomtowners strategy is a pure area income play. They are usually mining or remote towns and communities that offer high salaries because without that as a draw card, no one would live there. We call this the 'lifestyle test', meaning that if you didn't have the high-paying job, would you still stay in the town? Usually not! So when the town is booming, most people rent rather than buy, because they don't see their long-term future here, which results in very strong rental yields of more than 7 per cent.

Investors it's suited to?

Passive or Pure investors. You just need to make sure your bank is happy to lend against these types of security in these locations.

Difficulty level?

Local knowledge is important in these areas because this strategy goes against the traditional investor thinking that we present in the other strategies. Land isn't in short supply in these towns, but the cost of building in them in terms of supply and labour is significant. Therefore the dwelling has more value than the land (remember the land-to-asset ratio earlier in the book?). This strategy is the other way around. Generally speaking, properties with broad appeal will attract greater rental interest and result in high occupancy, post the boom period.

Risk and time allocation level?

High risk for pure mining towns and high to medium risk for remote towns from a buy-and-hold perspective. Make no mistake, it's a challenging investment strategy but if you get it right it also carries great rewards. You'll need many, many, many hours of research to do it effectively, which will probably involve travelling to some of these areas around Australia to gain the local knowledge required to form an investment opinion. Remember locals are going to talk it up, especially the real estate agents, so go to the pub or RSL and ask the following question, – "What's going right or wrong with this place?" to get a true idea of its potential.

Price point?

For mining areas, you're looking at $350,000 upwards, with the more established areas offering prices around $650,000. In remote towns – wait for it – $150,000 can be the starting point!

Tax implications and when to buy?

Usually these properties are cash flow positive investments from day one. Timing's really important here because the property values grow quickly over a short period of time, then prices can be flat for extended periods, so all you get during this period is the great rental income. Warning: after real boom times we can guarantee that mining town property values will tank, maybe not back to prices of 20 years ago, but they do come down significantly if the mining sector slows. Remote towns don't do this quite so much, but don't think of a remote town as one that has 200 people in it, think of it as a larger town that is a long way (over 400 km or more) from the capital city in a state, but which still has a good and potentially a great diversified economy.

STRATEGY 16 – The Non-Aspirers

The Non-Aspirers strategy is about finding investment areas where rental demand is high. These areas are usually found in the outer-suburban ring and are populated by a high proportion of low-income earners and/or people of a low socio-economic demographic. This type of tenant represents a large proportion of the rental market, as they struggle to break into the housing market themselves, due to their personal and financial circumstances. We don't condone taking advantage of this group, but rather we offer these tenants rental terms based on market value to provide much needed properties to live in. Look for areas in the middle to outer ring of major capital cities or on the fringes of the city centres of large regional towns. They need to be better areas than the really low socio-economic pockets of the city/town. Look for the pockets of good housing, better than average schools and lower crime rates. You want to find somewhere within a kilometre or two of an upper-market location, with a price point at the entry level that in the future will attract a tenant who can afford it. Understand the mind of the renters and what they would be looking for, such as privacy, security, full-fencing and low-maintenance – no spas, pools or landscaped gardens required here.

Investors it's suited to?

Passive or Pure investors. It's similar to No Vacancies in that it's about controlling the asset for as little surplus money as possible. The strong rental yields will help your borrowing power and your ability to hold the investment if your own cash flows are tight but you still want to invest.

Difficulty level?

Understand the demographics, such as the type of workers, their education levels, income, employment rates and the household makeup. You'll need to apply yourself to get the knowledge required, and the key is to aim for a well-built and durable property, given the wear and tear it might receive. Furthermore, the tenant selection for these properties is very important. You want someone who is trustworthy and respectful of your asset.

Risk and time allocation level?

Moderate, due to the rental demand and lower cash flow risk. This strategy can take time to find the right location and then the right property if you're chasing a superior investment return. It's reasonably easy to find areas with low socio-demographic profiles and status, but the challenge is finding an area you hope will become middle class over time.

Price point?

In city areas, you're looking at the $200,000 to $400,000 range for units. For houses you are starting at $350,000 upwards. In regional areas, units from $150,000 and houses from $250,000.

Tax implications and when to buy?

Properties are neutrally geared or slightly negatively geared initially, with prospects of being positively geared within one to five years at worst. There's no need to time the market for this strategy, as there are always areas like these that attract really high yields. That being said, it's smart investing to buy when the area is about to commence an upswing in its property cycle. The more research you do, the better the result you'll get – especially if you are a borderless investor and hunt nationally.

Property income strategies

STRATEGY 17 – *The Double Up*

The aim is to produce additional income streams from the one property, so think of the classic model of a granny flat or bungalow and you get the drift as to how this one works. It could also be transforming a double storey dwelling into two homes. Let's say you find a property with a large basement or rumpus room area downstairs and turn it into a small studio with kitchenette and ensuite which you can lease out separate to the upstairs. This strategy is not about large-scale construction or a dual-occupancy set up, which requires a long and detailed council planning approval. Rather it's all about restructuring the home where possible (within planning guidelines) or adding accommodation that doesn't require arduous town planning work (that strategy comes later).

Identify areas that this type of accommodation is best suited for, such as where there are many international or local students. Close to a university is a great start. Also remember that these properties already exist. The current owners might have set their property up for either their ageing parents or for the older child who wanted their own space. Google search for key words such as 'dual income', 'granny flat', 'bungalow', etc., to find these types of properties, as they can sometimes be tricky to seek out. Make sure you investigate to see if the property has a permit for the two living spaces and also talk to local property managers and the university to see if there is strong demand for this type of accommodation in the area.

Investors it's suited to?

Passive investors for existing properties and Active investors for those looking to add new accommodation to an existing property. For the Active investor, the best results will come from using an existing property so you can accrue income immediately, with agreement from the tenants to gain access to undertake the works necessary.

Difficulty level?

Understanding tenancy regulations is a great start here in relation to fire regulations, insurance and permits. You may need to invest time and effort to build up your local knowledge by talking to the local council to find out what is required to be fully compliant with rules and regulations. Some building companies specialise in this type of work, and they should have a 'rules and regulations list' for the local council where you are potentially looking to do this.

Risk and time allocation level?

Medium risk, as you have the comfort that at least there is one dwelling on the land earning you some income. There is regulatory risk as highlighted above, plus in some cases property managers might not be willing to manage this second accommodation, so you'll have to self-manage the tenants and their issues. Naturally, it will take up a lot of time to find an acceptable property and then to do all the extra bits needed to 'double up' the income. There's a great cash flow outcome though if you do get it right!

Price point?

Upwards of $400,000 in the city fringe and moving higher near universities and closer into the CBD areas.

Tax implications and when to buy?

The best properties will be positively geared or neutral at worst. If a property is negatively geared, that will be the result of putting a new granny flat or bungalow on the site. Yet the positives of this will be the depreciation you can claim. You won't need to time the market for this strategy, you just need to find the right property. Furthermore, it's less aggressive than some of the other income strategies, like renting a property bedroom by bedroom.

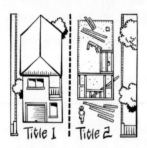

STRATEGY 18 – The Slice and Dice

The Slice and Dice strategy involves sub-dividing land into separate titles or a property into strata-titles. It can harvest equity out of the existing land and allow for an additional dwelling or several dwellings to be built for further income purposes. The separated land can also be sold off and the profit (less tax) can be used to pay down the loan on the property you still hold, making that property more cash flow positive. Hence a quick equity realisation plus the overall cash flow benefits make this strategy very appealing for some.

Find an area with a housing shortage that's in your investment price range. Don't risk buying a parcel of land where the demand for a smaller parcel of land is weak. Confirm that the block can be sub-divided. Make sure your next steps don't jeopardise the rental appeal and quality of living that the existing property offered, and make sure the new, sub-divided land is utilised to the best of its ability. This usually means the more dwellings you can get on it the better the overall return.

Investors it's suited to?

Active investors. It's going to be hands-on, even if you get professional help for some parts of this strategy. You'll need existing equity or savings and the ability to borrow two lots of funds if you are going to build the second property; the first funding will be to secure the existing property and the second will be for professional and government fees.

Difficulty level?

High. You need to assess your own level of knowledge and the sophistication of the property, and have the finance in place before embarking on a strategy like this, because quite simply it requires a lot of paperwork and understanding of the full process. Furthermore, any applications for changes to land title, use and building works, etc., need to go through an extensive administrative process that usually takes a long time – more than 12 months. If there are objections, you need to fight them in arbitration before you see any result for your extensive effort.

If you don't have a solid understanding of these processes then outsource to professionals or start small with a more conservative project first. If you have a town planning qualification or have extensive understanding of planning, you will be well placed, but you didn't need us to tell you that.

Risk and time allocation level?

High again. We call this an advanced style strategy because it contains many risks, further costs and cash injections to realise the gains.

Price point?

In small regional areas the entry price points can start at $200,000, then about $25,000 to sub-divide the land. That sounds low risk right? Wrong, what if it takes ten years to sell the new land lot you recreated, and then the interest costs are more than the gain you make by the time you sell it? Be careful! In city locations sub-prime land from $500,000 can work, but prime land is upwards of $1 million to secure the site and then to complete the build will cost at least another $500,000 plus.

Tax implications and when to buy?

The potential positive cash flow outcome of this strategy will impact positively on your passive income if the project is completed successfully. With a project of this nature, it is critical to seek good tax advice as there are many, many tax considerations here. Don't start this strategy without seeking that advice first.

Timing the market doesn't play a big role, except if the land or one of the new properties is to be sold off (here again good tax advice is critical). It's hard to establish the numbers without solid ground work, therefore it's not a strategy that suits everyone.

Summary of income strategies	
No vacancy	The Boomtowners
Non-Aspirers	The Double Up
The Slice and Dice	

So there you have it, 18 strategies we know work that we use every day for our clients to provide them with tailored property wealth plans. They should work for you too! We firmly believe that regardless of what potential investment you're considering, it'll be covered off in one of these 18 strategies. That means that you now have a far better understanding of what's required in order to invest more effectively in property. As we've mentioned throughout this book, property wealth-building sits in a buyer beware marketplace, so you'll need to keep your wits about you when dealing with the variety of property 'professionals' that litter the market.

We don't conform to or endorse any unprofessional investment beliefs or strategies. We have a property investment committee comprising qualified advisers with decades of experience. All the strategies have been approved by us. So whether you're chasing income or capital growth, or a balanced combination of the two, you can be assured that each one has been assessed on its merits, risk profile and has a high probability of success if actioned correctly.

If you plan to go it alone, you just need to do your own due diligence to work out whether the financial risk is worth it – but this applies to any investment because there's no guarantee that you'll be able to achieve income or capital growth, or both.

Next up – putting strategy into action!

HOW TO EARN $2,000 A WEEK

10

Congratulations! You've made it to the most important chapter of all – this is where we show you how to earn $2,000 a week from your property investments. This will allow you to retire – if that is your preference – or at least give you the freedom to choose whether or not to continue working. We've spent the last chapter showing you our 18 top strategies and now it's time to see how to apply them to our range of demographic scenarios that will each yield that magical figure. And let's be clear – the scenarios will enable you to cover all your costs as well as control a multi-million-dollar property portfolio, which will continue to deliver a passive income of $2,000 a week well into the next generation. Sounds OK, doesn't it?

Over the years we've met very similar client types, and these case studies are based on the six most common investors who walk through our door every year (before we apply our own sophisticated modelling and advice). By presenting portfolios that represent our most typical clients, hopefully they will be relevant to you in one way or another and you can apply the same rules for your own situation. It goes back to our 'armchair philosophy' that anyone can create wealth if they have the right tools, the right approach and the best team helping them.

Another important aspect about our scenarios is that you don't need to start out as a millionaire to achieve the $2,000 a week target. As we outlined at the beginning of this book, we'll show you how typical Australian households can keep the money rolling in and make their dreams come true.

Having said that, we are conservative property investors and advisers by nature, so these case studies haven't been quickly dreamt up. They are based on the combined decades of experience and knowledge of our qualified advisers who make up a committee that is highly skilled in creating and developing tailored property wealth plans and solutions for our clients. We hope you can immediately identify with at least one of these scenarios, but even if you find yourself straddling between two, we've given you enough information to allow you to apply them to your own situation.

We should also mention that this section is not a one-size-fits-all solution. This is because every client is different and it's inappropriate – and impossible – to include everyone in the same basket. We've already discussed the benefits of working with a good property investment team that will create a tailored solution to suit your specific requirements, so we'd highly recommend you get some professional help to set it all up before you jump in. We've done the numbers though so you're getting the benefit of our wisdom!

As you read through the scenarios, you'll see that we've tried to make them as easy as possible for you to understand. If you're a regular reader of our articles and listener to our podcast – The Property Couch – and have watched our videos, you might already be familiar with one or two case studies, but essentially here we showcase a portfolio plan that we've created to suit a particular demographic. We show you the numbers straight up and you'll be able to understand them straightaway.

What are the scenarios?

We pressure-tested the household budgets and life circumstances of a cross-section of the community. We wanted the case studies to be realistic and based on potential real-life scenarios, otherwise they lose their effect. So without further ado, here are our six case studies for you:

→ **Rentvestor.** Our single person who is just dipping his or her toes into the investment market and stepping onto the property ladder for the first time

→ **DINKS.** 'Double income no kids'. This growing market usually comprises a mid-30s couple without children

→ **Couple with young kids.** This scenario is all about unlocking the equity in your home and putting it to work

→ **Older couple with older kids.** Making up for lost time; there's a bit to do here to make it work as you're starting a little later than most

→ **Empty-nesters.** These guys also fall into the 'making up for lost time' basket but we show you how it can still be done

→ **Divorcee.** Facing the tough challenges of raising a family on a single income. We show you how to protect yourself but provide growth at the same time.

How did we do it?

The case studies in this book have been developed using our professional advisory skills and our proprietary software called the Property Wealth Planning Simulator. The simulator was actually developed out of a need to help our own families make important property investment decisions, and to make some sense of the complexities of cash flows, offset accounts, taxation and multiple loan accounts, growth and yield forecasts and projections. Many years ago now, we were finding all of this very difficult to understand, let alone then trying to model future plans and the cash flow needed to ensure we could achieve what we wanted to achieve personally and financially without making any big fundamental or financial mistakes.

With the help of one of our business partners, Michael Pope, we spent a period of two years developing our projection and forecasting modelling software package. This software is specifically designed for people who want to build multiple property portfolios to provide themselves with a self-funding retirement income.

Today, the program has helped us develop more than $750 million worth of property investment plans for our clients and has also helped Ben win the Property Investment Adviser of the Year award for the last two years running – 2014 and 2015.

To best understand our case studies you need to understand all of the moving parts. There are a lot when you are striving for a true and accurate indication of current and future cash flow and wealth creation outcomes using a simulator on modellings, assumptions, forecasts and projections. We're really pleased to share with you the framework and assumptions we used to help us build this wonderful software program and all the considerations within it, so that when you are doing your own modelling you will know what variables and assumptions to use in your models.

Figure 16: Money and wealth accumulation model

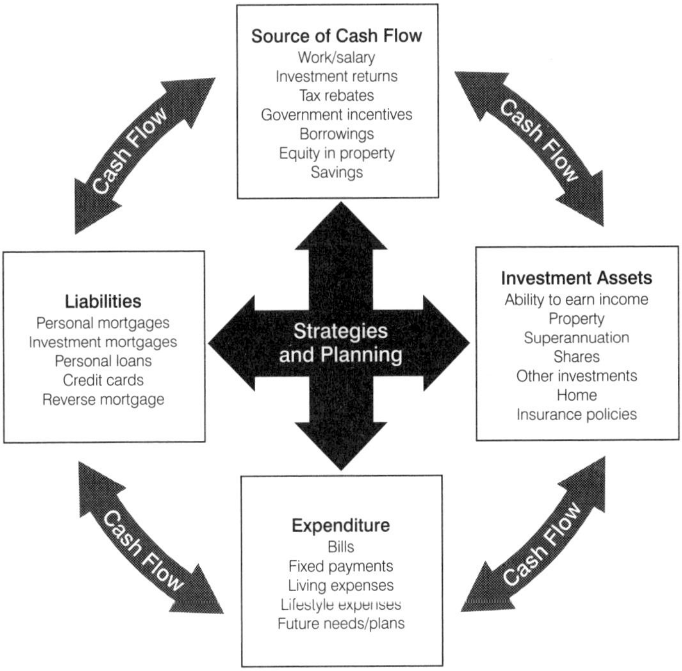
Source of Cash Flow
Work/salary
Investment returns
Tax rebates
Government incentives
Borrowings
Equity in property
Savings
Cash Flow
Cash Flow
Liabilities
Personal mortgages
Investment mortgages
Personal loans
Credit cards
Reverse mortgage
Strategies and Planning
Investment Assets
Ability to earn income
Property
Superannuation
Shares
Other investments
Home
Insurance policies
Cash Flow
Cash Flow
Expenditure
Bills
Fixed payments
Living expenses
Lifestyle expenses
Future needs/plans

The list below shows 'variables' and 'assumptions' to consider when modelling sophisticated money and wealth outcomes :

- Current salary and wages income
- Current other income
- Current taxation rates
- Current spending levels
- Current bill payment amounts
- Current value of family home
- Current savings
- Current superannuation balances
- Current superannuation contributions
- Current value of investments
- Current investment expenses
- Current investment yield returns
- Current borrowings
- Current interest rates
- Current rental yields
- Current value investment property/s
- Current property management fees
- Current maintenance expenses
- Current occupancy rates
- Current property investment expenses
- Current loan payment amounts
- Future salary and wages income
- Future other income
- Future taxation rates
- Future spending levels
- Future bill payment amounts
- Future value of family home
- Future savings
- Future superannuation balances
- Future superannuation contributions
- Future investment growth rates
- Future investment expenses
- Future investment yield returns
- Future borrowings
- Future interest rates

- Future rental yields
- Future property value growth rates
- Future property management fees
- Future maintenance expenses
- Future occupancy rates
- Future property investment expenses
- Future loan payment amounts
- Expected one-off lump sum incomes
- Expected one-off expenditures
- ATO income-variation impacts
- Future spending variations
- Depreciation cash flow add-backs
- Short-term income variations
- Long-term income variations
- Short-term expense variations
- Long-term expense variations
- Future property purchase expenses
- Future new loan balances
- Future land tax commitments
- Constant income monitoring
- Constant expenditure monitoring
- Regular investment performance reviews
- Regular investment performance adjustments
- Regular provisioning – income adjustment
- Regular provisioning – expenditure adjustment
- Regular adjustment variables percentage
- Regular review of assumptions percentages
- Your discipline to make it happen

When you think about it, this framework is absolutely the way it should be. As we've mentioned, property investing is a business and just like any business you need to create a business plan to become what you plan to become. All sound businesses make financial projections – you wouldn't see BHP-Billiton building a mine without a detailed financial and feasibility assessment – and that's why they are so successful, they have a plan. Use the same approach so you don't embark on building your $2,000 per week passive income without a game plan.

What are the assumptions?

To help you understand the level of detail that goes into these models without causing you a panic attack, it's important we highlight for you the general assumptions we've made within each case study:

→ All income is forecast to grow at 3 per cent p.a.
→ All expenditure is forecast to grow at 3 per cent p.a.
→ Employer superannuation guarantee (SG) contributions are 9.5 per cent of gross wages
→ Savings in the bank earn interest of 3 per cent p.a.
→ All existing and new lending is assumed to be incurring 6 per cent interest costs
→ Superannuation returns are assumed at 6 per cent p.a.
→ All property acquisition costs are set at 6 per cent of the purchase price
→ Taxation rates are current as at 2015-16 settings, indexing at 3 per cent p.a.
→ The ongoing cost of holding and maintaining the property in good letting order is 1.5 per cent of initial purchase costs – increasing at 3 per cent p.a.

→ Property management fees are 7.7 per cent
→ Occupancy rates are set at 92 per cent (assumed vacant for four weeks of each year)
→ No depreciation has been assumed in the modelling of any purchased property.

It should be no surprise that our key vehicle to generating our $2,000-a-week passive income is property. We're definitely not anti-shares or anti-traditional superannuation or anti-business; in fact, our firm actively provides advisers in all of these asset classes. But as we've clearly shown in this book our skillsets and qualifications are property-based and we have fine-tuned our knowledge over decades as property investors and property advisers.

Property is a tangible and easy-to-understand investment that will always be worth something as bricks and mortar. Furthermore, the banks love it, because they will lend to a higher loan-to-value ratio and at a lower interest rate than any other asset class they take as the security.

Finally, it's impossible to know where every one of the investment properties will actually be bought, considering that these are projections over the next decade and we don't know where the market will be headed. But we are confident that the properties do exist now in the current market, so we have every confidence that our scenarios will work in the future.

So here we go! We hope that these case studies will show you that even with different financial situations, following a set and proven process and formula for success will enable you to achieve the fantastic result of becoming a self-funded retiree!

CASE STUDY 1: Single (Rentvestor)

Meet Adam, age 25 (born 1990). You may have seen this term 'rentvestor' in the media lately; it's a hybrid of rent and investor. We're big fans of it because it neatly sums up the emerging market of young people choosing to rent in the inner city and buying an investment property in a more affordable suburb. Adam rents in a location he wants to live in, but where he can't afford to buy – so he's smart. Instead of waiting a long time, saving and saving so he can one day buy into the market where he wants to live, he's decided he's going to invest in property and keep renting. He's worked out that if he took out a large mortgage on a property to live in, he would be paying a lot more in loan repayments than what he pays in rent to live in this area. So instead, his plan is to put this money into several investment properties and he can have the people who rent them and some tax refunds help him pay them off over time and build a $2,000 per week passive income for his retirement.

Let's take a look at his current financials to paint a better picture:

Income

Adam currently earns $70,000 p.a. gross, and after tax and Medicare his net income is $54,303. His employer pays SG of $554 per month into his superannuation fund.

Outgoings

Now let's take a look at his expenses. His monthly bills and spending total $31,880 over the year.

Current Cash Flow Position	Monthly	Annually
Total Income	$4,525	$54,303
Total Expenses	$2,657	$31,880
Cash flow Surplus/Deficit	$1,869	$22,423

But that doesn't paint the whole picture. Adam has some assets contributing to his net worth and some liabilities reducing it. Adam's only liability is $500 owing on his credit card, so his current net worth position is:

Assets	Value
Securable Assets: Bank savings	$52,000
Unsecured Assets: Household effects, car and super	$61,000
Total Assets	$113,000
Total Liabilities	$500
Current Net Worth	$112,500

It's pretty obvious with this net worth position that Adam needs to do something. Other than the cash, which might earn some interest in the bank, the other assets he owns will actually depreciate in value over time and his savings and projected superannuation come retirement are around $850,000. If Adam were to try to live off $2,000 per week his money would run out very quickly indeed.

Adam isn't happy with this and has sought help and advice to build a plan to buy a series of investment properties over this journey that will turn his current situation on its head. The good news for Adam is that he has time on his side given his age, and he also wants to achieve his target earlier than the standard retirement age of 65. He is hoping to hit his $2,000 per week passive income at the young retirement age of 55 in 2045.

That being said, he also has to factor in some future costs to his household, which include replacing his car every 10 years and given he is going to invest in property and use lenders mortgage insurance (LMI), these costs also need to be accounted for:

Future Expenditure	Amount	Frequency	Date
Mortgage Insurance	$3,200	Once off	March 2016
Mortgage Insurance	$6,200	Once off	March 2020
Car Purchase	$20,000	Once off	June 2022
Car Purchase	$20,000	Once off	June 2032
Car Purchase	$20,000	Once off	June 2042

Investment property portfolio strategy

Here is our proposed investment strategy for Adam.

Investment Property 1

Present Value Purchase Price: $250,000
Purchase Timing: March 2016
Ownership Structure: Adam

Capital Growth p.a	Yield p.a.
5.00%	6.00%

Area/Location Strategy/ies	Property Selection Strategy/ies
No Vacancies	Scarce Diamond – Regional
The Non-Aspirer	Reliable and Durable
Boomtowners	Shoulder Rider
	Slice and Dice – Regional

Investment Property 2

Future Value Purchase Price: $441,867
    (Present Value Price $350,000)
Purchase Timing: March 2020
Ownership Structure: Adam

Capital Growth p.a.	Yield p.a.
6.00%	5.00%

Area/Location Strategy/ies	Property Selection Strategy/ies
Waver Rider	Reliable and Durable
Changing Places/Changing Faces	Scarce Diamond
The City Fling	Ugly Duckling
No Vacancies	Shoulder Rider

Investment Property 3

Future Value Purchase Price:	$744,748
	(Present Value Price $450,000)
Purchase Timing:	March 2024
Ownership Structure:	Adam

Capital Growth p.a.	Yield p.a.
6.50%	4.50%

Area/Location Strategy/ies	Property Selection Strategy/ies
Proven Performer	The Piggy Backer
Changing Places/Changing Faces	Reliable and Durable
Wave Rider	Scarce Diamond – Regional
City Fling	Ugly Duckling

Summary

Description	Target Purchase Price	Target Date	Target Growth	Target Yield
Residential Property 1	$250,000	Mar 2016	5.00%	6.00%
Residential Property 2	$441,867	Mar 2020	6.00%	5.00%
Residential Property 3	$744,748	Mar 2024	6.50%	4.50%

Below is the lending story associated with building this portfolio of properties. It's worth pointing out that when forecasting the purchase of each property you must also factor in borrowing a higher amount of money, which still needs to be paid off over the journey to allow that passive income to hit your back pocket and not the bank's.

Description	Loan Amount	As At	Monthly* Repayment	Loan Type
Loan for Property 1	$228,200	March 2016	$1,141	Int Only
Loan for Property 2	$405,508	March 2020	$2,028	Int Only
Loan for Property 3	$789,433	March 2024	$3,947	Int Only

*We assume a 6% interest rate on each loan

The future looks bright...

The table overleaf provides an excellent insight into the value of Adam's growing portfolio and the debt being paid down over time. *(It does look a little surreal when you see the potential value of the assets over a very long period of time, but that is the power of compounding interest, based on the value growth projections we estimated within the plan, which comes from historical growth rate returns that have occurred over the past 30 plus years!)* The weekly rent being collected will create the passive income Adam is after. If you are paying attention you will see the debt level actually increases after 30 years, which is caused by the fact that Adam doesn't yet have access to his superannuation. He needs to wait another five years before he can access this and when he does he can then pay down the debt and enjoy the spoils.

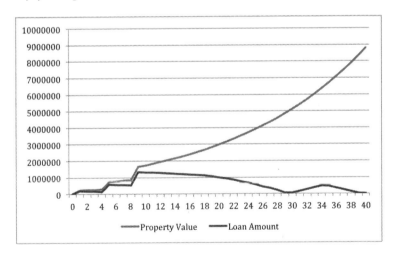

The fruits of Adam's labour are evident in the projections and forecast outcomes if Adam stays true to this plan. His rentvesting strategy will give him the flexibility to move around, rent and live where he likes, in the knowledge his property portfolio will grow over time and, hopefully, deliver the six figure passive investment returns for his efforts. You can see that by accumulating his assets he will successfully be able to reach $2,000 per week passive income, as well as retire at the younger age of 55 in 2045.

Description	Financial Position at			
	Now 2016	10 Years 2026	20 Years 2036	Retirement 2045
Savings and Super	$73,000	$130,654	$385,030	$851,051
Investment Property	–	$1,740,824	$2,979,881	$5,112,976
Other Investments	–	–	–	–
Total Investment Assets	–	$1,740,824	$2,979,881	$5,112,976
Total Assets	$73,000	$1,871,478	$3,364,911	$5,964,028
Total Debt	–	$1,312,752	$993,318	$0
Net Worth	$73,000	$558,726	$2,371,592	$5,964,028
Nest Egg (Investments)	$73,000	$558,726	$2,371,592	$5,964,028
Nest Egg (In Present Value Terms)		$415,745	$1,313,093	$2,529,799

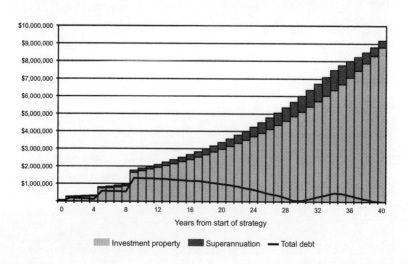

Years from start of strategy

▨ Investment property ▦ Superannuation — Total debt

CASE STUDY 2: DINKS

Meet Brian and Claire; our mid-thirties couple without kids. They fit the perfect DINKS profile – 'Double Income No Kids' – which you also may have read about in the media. There are more and more DINKS entering the market. Like many in this category, Brian and Claire have chosen not to have their own family as they are keen to retire early instead and live off their passive income. They have their family home locked away, as well as some equity to leverage from, which means their future situation looks very promising. As such, they are striving to be heading into retirement in 2042 at the tender ages of 55 and 54 respectively.

Let's take a look at their current financials to paint a better picture:

Income

Brian's gross income is $72,000 p.a. and Claire's is $78,000 p.a. After tax and Medicare Brian's net income is $55,615 and Claire's is $59,543. Their employer SG is $1,188 per month paid into their super funds.

Outgoings

Now let's take a look at their expenses. Their monthly bills and spending total $57,500 over the year.

Mortgage

Secured against their home is a mortgage of $300,000 with an interest rate of 5 per cent and a principal and interest repayment of $1,610 per month.

Current Cash Flow Position	Monthly	Annually
Total Income	$9,596	$115,156
Total Expenses	$4,792	$57,500
Mortgage Payments	$1,610	$19,326
Cash Flow Surplus	$3,194	$38,330

As you have heard us bang on about in this book, cash flow management is absolutely critical to manage the leverage you undertake when you build up your property portfolio. This case study is one example of taking control and managing that cash flow. Basically, the plan for Brian and Claire is to switch their loan over to an interest-only loan on their current home mortgage, which as we see will release an extra $360 per month to support any investment mortgages planned as they acquire their property investment portfolio.

Restructured Cash Flow Position	Monthly	Annually
Total Income	$9,596	$115,156
Total Expenses	$4,792	$57,500
Mortgage Payments	$1,250	$15,000
Cash flow Surplus	$3,555	$42,656

Here is their assets and liabilities story:

Assets	Value
Bank savings	$50,000
Household effects	$55,000
Superannuation	$180,000
Home	$550,000
Total assets	$835,000
Liabilities	**Value**
Credit Card	$750
Mortgage	$300,000
Total Assets	**$835,000**
Total Liabilities	$300,750
Current Net Worth	$534,250

With two incomes that won't be interrupted by the raising of children, you can see that this couple has more surplus cash now and into the future. It's true that money makes money so those who choose not to have children – DINKS – simply have more surplus cash flow. Not only can they enjoy uninterrupted income but also they have no ongoing costs associated with housing, feeding and educating children.

Still, there are some future expenses that need to be factored in, such as a provision for starting some new hobbies from 2017 onwards, a special holiday and replenishing their cars over their journey:

Reason for Future Expenses	Amount	Frequency	Start
Allocation to New Hobbies	$10,000	Yearly	Sept 2017
Car Replacement	$30,000	Once off	June 2020
Special Holiday	$25,000	Once off	Jan 2022
Car Replacement	$30,000	Once off	June 2028
Car Replacement	$30,000	Once off	June 2036

Investment property portfolio strategy

Now it's time to see what's possible for Brian and Claire.

Investment Property 1

Purchase Price:	$550,000 (Present Value: $550,000)
Purchase Timing:	March 2016
Ownership Structure:	Joint

Capital Growth p.a.	Yield p.a.
7.00%	4.25%

Area/Location Strategy/ies	Property Selection Strategy/ies
The Proven Performer	Reliable and Durable
Rare Earth	The Shoulder Rider
The Wave Rider	Scarce Diamond
Changing Places/Changing Faces	

Investment Property 2

Purchase Price:	$579,816 (Present Value: $480,000)
Purchase Timing:	March 2019
Ownership Structure:	Joint

Capital Growth p.a.	Yield p.a.
6.50%	4.50%

Area/Location Strategy/ies	Property Selection Strategy/ies
City Fling	Reliable and Durable
The Wave Rider	Ugly Duckling
Rare Earth	The Piggy Backer
The Proven Performer	

Investment Property 3

Purchase Price:	$925,981 (Present Value: $600,000)
Purchase Timing:	March 2022
Ownership Structure:	Joint

Capital Growth p.a.	Yield p.a.
7.50%	4.00%

Area/Location Strategy/ies	Property Selection Strategy/ies
Million Dollar Strip	Scarce Diamond
The Proven Performer	The Piggy Backer
Rare Earth	
City Fling	

Summary

Description	Target Purchase Price	Target Date	Target Growth	Target Yield
Residential Property 1	$550,000	Mar 2016	7.00%	4.25%
Residential Property 2	$579,816	Mar 2019	6.50%	4.50%
Residential Property 3	$925,981	Mar 2022	7.50%	4.00%

Opposite is the lending story associated with building this portfolio of properties, and it only takes three investment properties!

Description	Loan Amount	As At	Monthly* Repayment	Loan Type
Mortgage	$300,000	March 2016	$1,250	Int Only
Personal Buffer – Car Provision	$50,000	March 2016	$250	Int Only
Loan for Property 1	$583,000	March 2016	$2,915	Int Only
Loan for Property 2	$614,605	March 2019	$3,073	Int Only
Loan for Property 3	$981,540	March 2022	$4,908	Int Only

*We assume a 6% interest rate on each loan

It only took three investment properties...

With just three investment properties, all with capital growth as the major focus, Brian and Claire can get the job done at such an early age. In fact, this couple could buy more and build themselves a bigger portfolio if they wished.

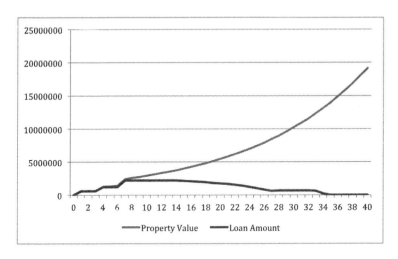

What we like about this strategy is that from a passive investment point of view, they only have three properties which makes their portfolio very easy to manage. Given the properties are expected to be bought in sound growth locations you'd like to think that the tenants these properties attract are respectful of the properties and will look after them. So there is little for Claire and Brian to do except get on with their international travels and enjoy the experiences that await them.

We've calculated that $104,000 in today's dollars is all ready for them to enjoy each year for the rest of their lives from 2042. You can also see that the value of their wealth continues to increase, so as time passes, they'll be worth even more.

| Description | Financial Position at | | | |
	Now 2016	10 Years 2026	20 Years 2036	Retirement 2043
Savings and Super	$180,000	$523,331	$1,267,827	$2,146,160
Investment Property	–	$2,913,546	$5,454,376	$8,466,124
Total Investment Assets	–	$2,913,546	$5,454,376	$8,466,124
Personal Assets	$550,000	$1,024,376	$1,907,900	$2,770,854
Total Assets	$730,000	$4,461,252	$8,630,104	$13,383,138
Total Debt	$250,000	$2,312,171	$1,779,915	$680,959
Net Worth	$480,000	$2,149,081	$6,850,189	$12,702,178
Nest Egg (Investments)	-$70,000	$1,124,706	$4,942,289	$9,931,325
Nest Egg (In Present Value Terms)		$836,887	$2,736,425	$4,470,974

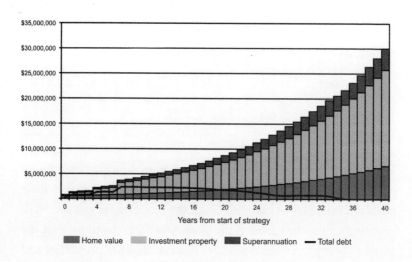

Who's paying attention? What appears to be quite 'interesting' in the above chart which predicts out beyond retirement to 2046 is that the debt increases in value from the years 2043 ($680,959) to 2046 ($742,394), yet their superannuation and savings total over $2.146 million. So why haven't we just paid the debt out?

This is because the vast majority of this is actually their superannuation balance and under current laws this money can't be touched until they turn 60 years old. So as they are retiring at 55 and 54 years of age, why wait to get access to super? Instead, they're actually using the money they have stored up in their offset accounts to enjoy their retirement and when they do hit 60, they can retire this debt and retain all properties as their retirement rent roll. Nice hey!

CASE STUDY 3: Couple with young kids

Meet David and Liz; a couple in their late 30s. They have two children: Francis, who's six years old and his sister Grace, who's four years old. Francis is in primary school and Grace is finishing up in child care and about to start primary school. David works full time and Liz works part time. They currently hold no investment properties but are looking to build up a property portfolio to assist them in achieving a retirement date target of 2037 and generating a $2,000 per week passive income. This will see David retire at the age of 60 and Liz at the age of 59.

Let's take a look into their current financials to paint a better picture of their situation:

Income

David's wage is $95,000 p.a. and Liz's is $56,000 p.a. After calculating share income, tax and Medicare, David's net income is $70,552 and Liz's is $45,293. Their combined employer SG is $1,195 per month paid into their super funds.

Outgoings

Now let's take a look at their expenses. Their monthly bills and spending total $58,870 over the year.

Mortgage

Secured against their home is a mortgage of $320,000 with an interest rate of 5 per cent and a principal and interest monthly repayment of $1,718.

Current Cash Flow Position	Monthly	Annually
Total Income	$9,654	$115,845
Total Expenses	$4,906	$58,870
Fixed Payments	$1,718	$20,614
Cash Flow Surplus/Deficit	$3,030	$36,361
Restructured Cash Flow Position	**Monthly**	**Annually**
Total Income	$9,654	$115,845
Total Expenses	$4,906	$58,870
Fixed Payments	$1,420	$17,040
Cash Flow Surplus/Deficit	$3,328	$39,935

Here is their Assets and Liabilities story:

Assets	Value
Bank savings	$36,000
Shares	$22,000
Household effects	$85,000
Superannuation	$264,200
Home	$650,000
Liabilities	
Credit Card	$1,150
Mortgage	$320,000
Summary	
Total Assets	$1,057,200
Total Liabilities	$321,150
Current Net Worth	$736,050

With two young kids, their education costs will increase as they head into secondary school, before those costs end and eventually their kids leave home. But the provision for their kids continues as they set aside some savings for special holidays and also a couple of very special wedding gifts. In addition, they plan some renovations for their current home. These future changes to expenditure are outlined below.

Reason	Amount	Frequency	Time Period
Special Family Holiday	$15,000	Once off	July 2020
Increase In Education Fees (High School)	$5,000	Yearly	2022 to 2028
Replacement Car	$35,000	Once off	June 2023
Increase In Education Fees (High School)	$5,000	Yearly	2024 to 2030
Replacement Car	$20,000	Once off	June 2025
Special Family Holiday	$15,000	Once off	July 2025
Home Renovations	$30,000	Once off	Sept 2028
Replacement Car	$35,000	Once off	June 2033
Replacement Car	$20,000	Once off	June 2035
Contribution to Wedding	$15,000	Once off	Sept 2040
Contribution to Wedding	$15,000	Once off	Sept 2042

Investment property portfolio strategy

It's now time to see what's possible for David and Liz.

Investment Property 1

Purchase Price: $500,000 (Present Value: $500,000)
Purchase Timing: April 2016
Ownership Structure: David

Capital Growth p.a.	Yield p.a.
7.00%	4.00%

Area/Location Strategy/ies	Property Selection Strategy/ies
The Proven Performer	The Piggy Backer
Rare Earth	Scarce Diamond
Million Dollar Strip	Reliable and Durable
City Fling	The Shoulder Rider

Investment Property 2

Purchase Price: $359,552 (Present Value $320,000)
Purchase Timing: March 2018
Ownership Structure: Joint Ownership

Capital Growth p.a.	Yield p.a.
6.00%	5.00%

Area/Location Strategy/ies	Property Selection Strategy/ies
Changing Places/Changing Faces	Reliable and Durable
City Fling	The Shoulder Rider
No Vacancies	Ugly Duckling
The Wave Rider	

Investment Property 3

Purchase Price:	$656,614 (Present Value $450,000)
Purchase Timing:	March 2022
Ownership Structure:	David

Capital Growth p.a.	Yield p.a.
6.50%	4.50%

Area/Location Strategy/ies	Property Selection Strategy/ies
The Proven Performer	Scarce Diamond
Rare Earth	The Piggy Backer
Million Dollar Strip	The Shoulder Rider
Changing Places/Changing Faces	Reliable and Durable

Investment Property 4

Purchase Price:	$284,420 (Present Value $200,000)
Purchase Timing:	September 2024
Ownership Structure:	Joint Ownership

Capital Growth p.a.	Yield p.a.
4.50%	6.50%

Area/Location Strategy/ies	Property Selection Strategy/ies
No Vacancies	Reliable and Durable
The Boomtowners	The Shoulder Rider
Non-Aspirers	Ugly Duckling
The Wave Rider	

Summary

Description	Target Purchase Price	Target Date	Target Growth	Target Yield
Investment Property 1	$500,000	Apr 2016	7.00%	4.00%
Investment Property 2	$359,552	Mar 2018	6.00%	5.00%
Investment Property 3	$656,614	Mar 2022	6.50%	4.50%
Investment Property 4	$284,420	Sep 2024	4.50%	6.50%

Below is the lending story associated with building this portfolio of properties:

Description	Loan Amount	As At	Monthly* Repayment	Loan Type
Mortgage	$320,000	March 2016	$1,420	Int Only
Personal Buffer	$50,000	April 2016	$250	Int Only
Loan for Property 1	$530,000	April 2016	$2,650	Int Only
Loan for Property 2	$381,125	March 2018	$1,906	Int Only
Loan for Property 3	$696,011	March 2022	$3,480	Int Only
Loan for Property 4	$301,485	Sept 2024	$1,507	Int Only

*We assume a 6% interest rate on each loan

Four investment properties is our target

David and Liz's property portfolio strategy has a blend of growth assets mixed with a balanced and high-yielding asset, which we often refer to as a 'cash cow'. The timing of each type of purchase is important to understand, given theirs will be when the kids are at secondary school and the household cash flow is less. It's a case of acting sensibly and within one's means during this time, which is why we have recommended higher-yielding properties to ensure the household cash flow position is not too constrained.

You should also pick up that we have used some of the equity they have in their family home to provide a personal buffer loan in the event of any emergencies. This buffer means David and Liz don't need to panic, as this money buys them some time to work things through and get back on their feet so to speak.

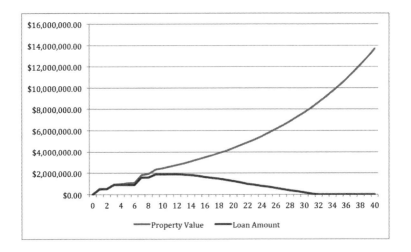

The graph above tells a story of the value of the portfolio growing nicely and the overall debt being paid off. So the full picture of how David and Liz will achieve a passive income of $2,000 per week in 2037 looks like this:

	Financial Position at			
	Now	10 Years	20 Years	Retirement
Description	2016	2026	2036	2037
Savings and Super	$264,200	$680,106	$1,555,169	$1,778,465
Investment Property	–	$2,475,400	$4,360,333	$4,885,538
Other Investments	$22,000	$37,579	$64,191	$67,721
Total Investment Assets	$22,000	$2,512,979	$4,424,524	$4,953,259
Personal Assets	$650,000	$1,210,626	$2,254,791	$2,399,474
Total Assets	$936,200	$4,403,711	$8,234,484	$9,131,198
Total Debt	$284,000	$2,004,417	$1,317,447	$1,045,478
Net Worth	$652,200	$2,399,294	$6,917,037	$8,085,720
Nest-Egg (Investments)	$2,200	$1,188,668	$4,662,246	$5,686,246
Nest-Egg (In Present Value Terms)		$884,481	$2,581,372	$3,056,637

As with the other case studies in this book that there is still some debt outstanding at retirement. In David and Liz's case, this remains over $1.045 million, which when you look at it in isolation appears to be a lot of outstanding money. But at the same time they have over $9.131 million in total assets.

In this case study, David and Liz haven't opted to sell any of the four investment properties they own. Instead, they keep them because they are generating enough income to pay their passive income of $2,000 per week. Plus they are also generating surplus income over and above this amount to make the repayments on the outstanding loan balance. The wealth projection graph below shows that over time this debt will be completely paid out in full and David and Liz get to keep all four properties to generate even more than $2,000 income per week. A fantastic result!

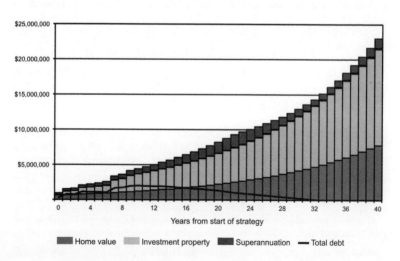

CASE STUDY 4: Older couple with older kids

Meet Harvey and Ingrid, a couple in their mid 40s. They have three children all in their teens: Jessica who's 18, but plans to hang at home for a few more years yet; Kyle who's 16 years old; and finally Lauren who's 14 years old. To date, Harvey and Ingrid's life has revolved around their kids and giving them the best start in life.

Little did they know that they could have been investing some 10 years earlier, but like many, their lack of knowledge has hindered them to believe they were not in a position to invest. In fact, their decision to wait has potentially cost them hundreds of thousands of dollars in future lost wealth. Starting at their age will result in them working a little longer to hit the magic $2,000 per week in income at their retirement. Anyway they can't go back in time, so all they can do is learn from it and know they are ready to do something about it.

Given the ages of the kids and the fact they're pretty well grown up, both Harvey and Ingrid work full time and as such they bring in very good combined household gross salaries of $210,000. As mentioned, there are no investment properties in the mix just yet, but that is about to change as they have a strong equity position, thanks to having owned their home for so long. While only paying the minimum off their mortgage, their cash flows are very strong.

Their retirement date target is January 2035, when Harvey will be 65 and Ingrid will be 64. Once again, the target income we wish to generate is $2,000 per week as a self-funded retirement outcome.

Let's take a look into their current financials to paint a better picture of their situation:

Income

Harvey's wage is $120,000 p.a. and Ingrid's is $90,000 p.a. After share income, tax and Medicare, Harvey's net income is $85,253 and Ingrid's is $67,258. Their combined employer SG is $1,663 per month paid into their super funds.

Outgoings

Now let's take a look at their expenses. Their monthly bills and spending total $86,936 over the year.

Mortgage

Secured against their home is a mortgage of $410,000 with an interest rate of 5 per cent and a principal and interest monthly repayment of $2,201.

Current Cash Flow Position	Monthly	Annually
Total Income	$12,709	$152,511
Total Expenses	$7,245	$86,936
Fixed Payments	$2,201	$26,412
Cash Flow Surplus/Deficit	$3,264	$39,163
Restructured Cash Flow Position	**Monthly**	**Annually**
Total Income	$12,709	$152,511
Total Expenses	$7,245	$86,936
Fixed Payments	$1,685	$20,220
Cash Flow Surplus/Deficit	$3,780	$45,355

Here is their Assets and Liabilities story:

Assets	Value
Bank savings – Offset Account	$73,000
Shares	$10,000
Household effects	$130,000
Superannuation	$386,000
Home	$850,000

Liabilities

Credit Card	$Nil
Mortgage	$410,000

Summary

Total Assets	$1,449,000
Total Liabilities	$410,000
Current Net Worth	$1,039,000

With three older kids, the cost of running their household will actually reduce as each child leaves home. We have factored in that one of the kids will leave home in early 2018, then another in early 2022 and then the final child in early 2025. With each of these events, an additional $350 per month will go back into the household cash flows. Other future changes to expenditure are outlined below and reflect a realistic picture of one-off and regular changes in expenditure over their journey.

Reason	Amount	Frequency	Date
Help to Buy Child 1 First Car	$10,000	Once off	Dec 2015
Help to Buy Child 2 First Car	$10,000	Once off	March 2017
Replacement Car	$40,000	Once off	May 2017
First Child Leaves Home	-$350	Monthly	Feb 2018
Special Family Holiday	$25,000	Once off	July 2019
Help to Buy Child 3 First Car	$10,000	Once off	Sept 2019
Second Child Leaves Home	-$350	Monthly	Feb 2022
Replacement Car	$20,000	Once off	June 2022
Home Renovations	$80,000	Once off	Oct 2022
25th Wedding Anniversary Special holiday	$20,000	Oncc off	Fcb 2024
Third Child Leaves Home	-$350	Monthly	Feb 2025
Replacement Car	$45,000	Once off	June 2027
Wedding Gift	$10,000	Once off	Nov 2027
Wedding Gift	$10,000	Once off	Nov 2029
Wedding Gift	$10,000	Once off	Nov 2031
Replacement Car	$20,000	Once off	June 2032
Replacement Car	$45,000	Once off	June 2034

Investment property portfolio strategy

It's now time to see what's possible for Harvey and Ingrid.

Investment Property 1

Purchase Price:	$700,000 (Present Value: $700,000)
Purchase Timing:	April 2016
Ownership Structure:	Harvey

Capital Growth p/a	Yield p/a
7.00%	4.00%

Area/Location Strategy/ies	Property Selection Strategy/ies
The Proven Performer	Scarce Diamond
Rare Earth	Reliable and Durable
Million Dollar Strip	The Piggy Backer

Investment Property 2

Purchase Price:	$585,750 (Present Value: $550,000)
Purchase Timing:	September 2017
Ownership Structure:	Joint Ownership

Capital Growth p.a.	Yield p.a.
6.50%	4.50%

Area/Location Strategy/ies	Property Selection Strategy/ies
Rare Earth	Reliable and Durable
The Proven Performer	The Shoulder Rider
City Fling	Ugly Duckling
The Wave Rider	Size Matters

Investment Property 3

Purchase Price:	$476,406 (Present Value: $400,000)
Purchase Timing:	October 2019
Ownership Structure:	Joint Ownership

Capital Growth p.a.	Yield p.a.
6.00%	5.00%

Area/Location Strategy/ies	Property Selection Strategy/ies
City Fling	Scarce Diamond
The Wave Rider	Size Matters
Changing Places/Changing Faces	Reliable and Durable
No Vacancies	The Piggy Backer

Investment Property 4 (Optional)

Purchase Price:	$316,330 (Present Value: $250,000)
Purchase Timing:	September 2022
Ownership Structure:	Ingrid

Capital Growth p.a.	Yield p.a.
4.00%	7.00%

Area/Location Strategy/ies	Property Selection Strategy/ies
No Vacancies	Reliable and Durable
The Boomtowners	The Shoulder Rider
Non-Aspirers	Ugly Duckling
The Wave Rider	The Piggy Backer

Summary

Description	Target Purchase Price	Target Date	Target Growth	Target Yield
Investment Property 1	$700,000	Apr 2016	7.00%	4.00%
Investment Property 2	$585,750	Sep 2017	6.50%	4.50%
Investment Property 3	$476,406	Oct 2019	6.00%	5.00%
Investment Property 4 (Optional)	$316,330	Sep 2022	4.00%	7.00%

Below is the lending story associated with building this portfolio of properties:

Description	Loan Amount	As At	Monthly* Repayment	Loan Type
Mortgage	$410,000	Mar 2016	$1,685	Int Only
Loan for Property 1	$742,000	Apr 2016	$3,710	Int Only
Loan for Property 2	$620,895	Sept 2017	$3,104	Int Only
Loan for Property 3	$504,991	Oct 2019	$2,525	Int Only
Loan for Property 4 (Optional)	$335,310	Sept 2022	$1,677	Int Only
Renovation Loan	$95,524	Oct 2022	$478	Int Only

*We assume a 6% interest rate on each loan

THE ARMCHAIR GUIDE TO PROPERTY INVESTING

Three investment properties are all that is needed, with one as an optional extra

Harvey and Ingrid's property portfolio strategy has a weighted focus on growth assets early and then an optional high-yielding property (a cash cow) at the end of the accumulation phase. This last property is optional to help with building up additional income to reduce the debt. It's not completely required, but if they are comfortable at that time to take on one more property then the long-term outcome is even greater. The timing is not too aggressive either, and it's important they feel comfortable with the process, securing a tenant and feeling happy overall that they are doing the right thing. Then they will be well placed to buy the second and the third property, and so on.

Once again, it's the use of their equity that has helped this family get into property investing. They borrowed 106 per cent of the value of each property using this equity, which enabled them to keep their current savings as a cash buffer. This is held in an offset account to look after the family's needs.

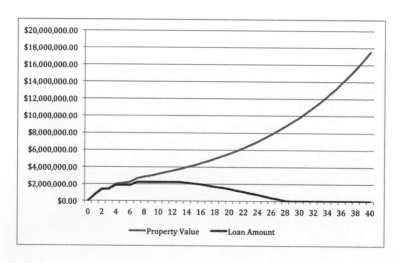

Another pleasing story shown above is the separation of value from the debt used to hold those properties. During the accumulation phase that debt is significant, but over time as the values of the properties increase, so too does the rent. When the kids leave home the surplus income gets stronger, which helps to pay down the debt completely over time, leaving the property portfolio for Harvey and Ingrid to pass onto the kids! (or they could just sell up and have an amazing retirement!).

		Financial Position at		
Description	Now 2016	10 Years 2026	Retirement 2035	20 Years 2036
Savings and Super	$386,000	$979,628	$2,029,420	$1,875,912
Investment Property	–	$3,165,109	$5,261,898	$5,569,204
Other Investments	$10,000	$17,081	$26,215	$29,178
Total Investment Assets	$10,000	$3,182,191	$5,288,112	$5,598,382
Personal Assets	$850,000	$1,583,126	$2,603,710	$2,948,573
Total Assets	$1,246,000	$5,744,945	$9,921,242	$10,422,867
Total Debt	$337,000	$2,484,352	$1,692,560	$1,496,309
Net Worth	$909,000	$3,260,593	$8,228,682	$8,926,558
Nest-Egg (Investments)	$59,000	$1,677,467	$5,624,972	$5,977,985
Nest-Egg (In Present Value Terms)		$1,248,193	$3,207,843	$3,309,865

Net worth and nest-egg are what we focus on in each case study. That's the true value or wealth that is being created by taking these risks and investing. In Harvey and Ingrid's case, 30 years into the future, their nest-egg figure is a crazy $10+ million, but then when you bring it back to present day terms it is at $4.3 million (factoring in the inflation of money), and it doesn't look that silly anymore. Property has always been a great hedge against inflation and this really highlights it.

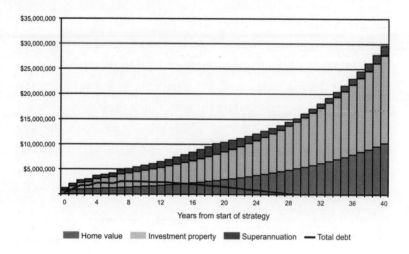

CASE STUDY 5: Empty-nesters

Meet Gary and Nancy, our empty-nester couple in their early 50s. Their kids have flown the coup and so they are really starting to put themselves first again. They need to build their nest-egg so they can enjoy what they hope will be a very long retirement full of new travels and experiences, while also being grandparents and spending time with their future grand kids.

Initially, they thought it might be too late for them to jump on the property investment ladder. Yes, we would have liked to see them some 20 years earlier, as it would have been a lot more 'relaxed' to build their property plan. But it is what it is and they have enjoyed their journey through life until now. Our job is to help them retire in a much better financial position than they are currently in, by helping them generate a $2,000 per week passive income for their life after work!

Their retirement date target is January 2031, when they will both be 68 years old. It's a little over the dream target of 65, but unfortunately that's what the impact of starting late can do and bear in mind we are chasing $2,000 per week of income. Naturally, if they decide they can live off less, then of course the strategy would adjust accordingly.

Let's take a look into their current financials to paint a better picture of their situation:

Income

Gary's wage is $87,000 p.a. and Nancy's is $52,000 p.a. After share income, tax and Medicare Gary's net income is $65,580 and Nancy's is $43,213. Their combined employer SG is $1,100 per month paid into their super funds.

Outgoings

Now let's take a look at their expenses. Their monthly bills and spending total $71,500 over the year.

Mortgage and credit cards

Secured against their home is a mortgage of $54,000 with an interest rate of 5 per cent and a principal and interest repayment of $290 over a 30-year term, plus $75 per month on the credit card with an outstanding balance of $900.

Current Cash Flow Position	Monthly	Annually
Total Income	$9,066	$108,793
Total Expenses	$5,958	$71,500
Fixed Payments	$365	$4,379
Cash flow Surplus/Deficit	$2,743	$32,914
Restructured Cash Flow Position	**Monthly**	**Annually**
Total Income	$9,066	$108,793
Total Expenses	$5,958	$71,500
Fixed Payments	$106	$1,272
Cash flow Surplus/Deficit	$3,002	$36,021

Here is their Assets and Liabilities story:

Assets	Value
Bank savings – Offset Account	$48,000
Shares	$30,000
Household effects	$120,000
Superannuation	$346,000
Home	$600,000
Liabilities	
Credit Card	$900
Mortgage	$54,000
Summary	
Total Assets	$1,115,000
Total Liabilities	$54,900
Current Net Worth	$1,060,100

Overall Gary and Nancy have been able to build up some super-annuation relative to their ages, but if you strip out the family home (and we all need to live somewhere) there isn't a lot of nest-egg to be able to generate the income they are looking for to have a carefree retirement. Factoring in the future expenditures such as the increase in the annual travel budget of $2,000, which is fair enough in pre-retirement, wise money management and asset selection are going to be important as they move into top gear in their wealth accumulation phase.

Reason	Amount	Frequency	Date
Reno Bathroom and Kitchen	$40,000	Once off	June 2017
Increase In Annual Holiday Budget	$2,000	Yearly	Jan 2020
Replacement of Car	$25,000	Once off	June 2024
Wedding Gift to Only Daughter	$20,000	Once off	March 2026
25th Wedding Anniversary	$15,000	Once off	Feb 2027
Replacement of Car	$25,000	Once off	June 2029

Investment property portfolio strategy

Let's see what we are able to do for this couple who aren't getting any younger…

Investment Property 1

Purchase Price:	$480,000 (Present Value: $480,000)
Purchase Timing:	May 2016
Ownership Structure:	Gary

Capital Growth p.a.	Yield p.a.
6.00%	5.00%

Area/Location Strategy/ies	Property Selection Strategy/ies
The Proven Performer	The Shoulder Rider
Changing Places/Changing Faces	Size Matters
City Fling	Reliable and Durable
No Vacancies	Ugly Duckling

THE ARMCHAIR GUIDE TO PROPERTY INVESTING

Investment Property 2

Purchase Price: $446,250 (Present Value: $425,000)
Purchase Timing: May 2017
Ownership Structure: Joint Ownership

Capital Growth p.a.	Yield p.a.
5.00%	6.00%

Area/Location Strategy/ies	Property Selection Strategy/ies
Changing Places/Changing Faces	Reliable and Durable
The Wave Rider	The Shoulder Rider
No Vacancies	Ugly Duckling
Non-Aspirers	Size Matters

Investment Property 3

Purchase Price: $382,209 (Present Value: $350,000)
Purchase Timing: May 2018
Ownership Structure: Gary

Capital Growth p.a.	Yield p.a.
4.50%	6.50%

Area/Location Strategy/ies	Property Selection Strategy/ies
No Vacancies	Ugly Duckling
The Wave Rider	Size Matters
Non-Aspirers	Reliable and Durable
The Boomtowners	The Piggy Backer

Investment Property 4

Purchase Price: $281,216 (Present Value: $250,000)
Purchase Timing: May 2019
Ownership Structure: Joint Ownership

Capital Growth p.a.	Yield p.a.
4.00%	7.00%

Area/Location Strategy/ies	Property Selection Strategy/ies
No Vacancies	Reliable and Durable
Non-Aspirers	Ugly Duckling
The Boomtowners	The Shoulder Rider
The Wave Rider	The Piggy Backer

Summary

Description	Target Purchase Price	Target Date	Target Growth	Target Yield
Investment Property 1	$480,000	May 2016	6.00%	5.00%
Investment Property 2	$446,250	May 2017	5.00%	6.00%
Investment Property 3	$382,209	May 2018	4.50%	6.50%
Investment Property 4	$281,216	May 2019	4.00%	7.00%

Below is the lending story associated with building this portfolio of properties:

Description	Loan Amount	As At	Rate	Monthly Repay.	Loan Type
Mortgage	$54,000	April 2016	6.00%	$30	Int Only
Credit Card	$900	April 2016	20.00%	$76	1 year
Loan for Property 1	$508,800	May 2016	6.00%	$2,544	Int Only
Loan for Property 2	$473,025	May 2017	6.00%	$2,365	Int Only
Loan for Property 3	$405,141	May 2018	6.00%	$2,026	Int Only
Loan for Property 4	$298,089	May 2019	6.00%	$1,490	Int Only

Four investment properties is the target for Gary and Nancy

There's no time like the present with this strategy. Gary and Nancy need to get moving to lock these properties away so that they'll do the lifting needed over the next 20+ years and beyond. The focus with this portfolio plan is to generate more yield quicker because Gary and Nancy need the passive rental income to kick in earlier and to mature quicker, due to lower cash flows and shorter timeframe to retirement. This is different to the growth-focused assets of previous case studies with a longer timeframe until retirement. Higher yielding properties will allow the portfolio to start to generate a surplus cash flow from the rent and help to keep control over the debt levels they have leveraged into. It's important to note that Gary and Nancy's decision to implement this plan comes with a willingness to take on the higher risk associated with debt at their age. To them, this is a calculated play and if it doesn't work over time they can simply exit the strategy, sell down the properties and pay off the loans.

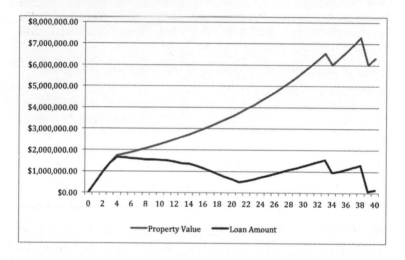

In the graph above we can see that there are two planned sales post retirement. This helps them pay down the debt levels, while also enables them to enjoy the $2,000 per week that's generated from the property from the time they retire in 2031. They can also service their remaining debt at that time.

		Financial Position at		
Description	Now 2016	10 Years 2026	Retirement 2031	20 Years 2036
Savings and Super	$346,000	$813,085	$1,190,061	$221,874
Investment Property	$	$2,272,085	$2,853,515	$3,587,492
Other Investments	$30,000	$51,244	$63,483	$87,533
Total Investment Assets	$30,000	$2,323,329	$2,916,998	$3,675,025
Personal Assets	$600,000	$1,117,501	$1,433,133	$2,081,346
Total Assets	$976,000	$4,253,914	$5,540,192	$5,978,245
Total Debt	$6,900	$1,525,221	$1,295,164	$622,934
Net Worth	$969,100	$2,728,694	$4,245,029	$5,355,311
Nest Egg (Investments)	$369,100	$1,611,193	$2,811,896	$3,273,965
Nest Egg (In Present Value Terms)		$1,198,879	$1,804,849	$1,812,715

It's 2016 and Gary and Nancy are set to retire in 2031, which is 15 years from now. The graph overleaf shows the accumulation phase over the first four years before it becomes all about debt retirement to generate the clear passive income they are striving for. At retirement, they use super and savings to further reduce debt. Yet from 2031, in today's dollar terms they are drawing $2,000 a week income in this model and this is seeing their debt levels increase, as per the solid line towards the bottom of the graph. This is by no means concerning because when they think it's time to cash in on one property they do that, which gives them a cash windfall after capital gains tax. Gary and Nancy live off that windfall before they sell a second property some four years later. This second sale effectively removes all the debt and they still have two properties that will continue to generate the passive income of over $100,000 a year for their retirement. Great going guys!

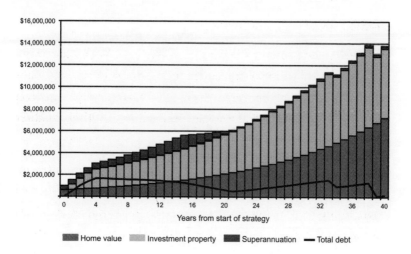

CASE STUDY 6: Divorcee

Olivia fell in love early in life, ah that young love! But as one grows and matures over time it's not uncommon to drift apart and have values and goals that don't align anymore. This is the case for Olivia and she now finds herself as a single mum with a beautiful daughter named Trudi, who's 15 years old.

Life is not easy for single mums and Olivia's story is no different. However, she's wise to money and keen to carve out a better financial future for herself and her daughter. She isn't across shares and finds that side of things a little too scary for her and her money. Instead, she is happy with good old-fashioned bricks and mortar. She also wants to educate herself and put a strategy and plan in place to see a better financial future materialise. Olivia understands it is going to require some tight budgeting and Money SMARTS to make it happen, but she's willing to put in the hard yards.

Olivia's retirement date target is January 2038, when she will be 65. Once again, this property wealth plan is targeting income of $2,000 per week as a self-funded retirement outcome.

Let's take a look into Olivia's current financials:

Income

Olivia's gross income is $89,000 p.a. After tax and Medicare her net income is $66,343 and her employer SG is $705 per month paid into her super fund.

Outgoings

Now let's take a look at her expenses. Monthly bills and spending total $40,700 over the year.

Mortgage

Secured against her home is a mortgage of $120,000 with an interest rate of 5 per cent and a principal and interest monthly repayment of $644.

Current Cash Flow Position	Monthly	Annually
Total Income	$5,529	$66,343
Total Expenses	$3,392	$40,700
Fixed Payments	$644	$7,730
Cash Flow Surplus/Deficit	$1,493	$17,913
Restructured Cash Flow Position	**Monthly**	**Annually**
Total Income	$5,529	$66,343
Total Expenses	$3,392	$40,700
Fixed Payments	$460	$5,520
Cash Flow Surplus/Deficit	$1,677	$20,123

Here is her Assets and Liabilities story:

Assets	Value
Bank savings	$28,000
Shares	$0
Household effects	$103,000
Superannuation	$172,000
Home	$680,000
Liabilities	
Credit Card	$0
Mortgage	$120,000
Summary	
Total Assets	$983,000
Total Liabilities	$120,000
Current Net Worth	$863,000

Olivia's current position is OK considering she has been single for more than five years after her divorce. That said, her super isn't going to carry her off into the sunset, even if she works for another 20 plus years. Quite simply, more needs to be done and leverage, combined with property, will provide the vehicle for Olivia.

As mentioned earlier, Olivia is going to need to run a tight ship with her spending, yet she still needs to live, keep the home liveable and provide for Trudi until she is able to leave the nest herself. In our model, it is assumed that Trudi will leave home at the age of 25.

Reason	Amount	Frequency	Start
Gift towards Trudi's First Car	$5,000	Once off	June 2018
Special 50th Holiday gift to self	$5,000	Once off	June 2023
Replacement Car	$20,000	Once off	June 2024
Trudi Leaves Home	-$350	Monthly	Jan 2025
Cosmetic Home Renovations	$15,000	Once off	April 2025
Wedding Gift for Trudi	$10,000	Once off	Nov 2030
Replacement Car	$20,000	Once off	June 2034
Replacement Car	$20,000	Once off	June 2044

Investment property portfolio strategy

It's now time to see what's possible for Olivia.

Investment Property 1

Purchase Price: $475,000 (Present Value: $475,000)
Purchase Timing: May 2016
Ownership Structure: Olivia

Capital Growth p.a.	Yield p.a.
6.00%	5.00%

Area/Location Strategy/ies	Property Selection Strategy/ies
The Proven Performer	Reliable and Durable
City Fling	The Shoulder Rider
Changing Places/Changing Faces	Size Matters
The Wave Rider	The Piggy Backer

Investment Property 2

Purchase Price: $369,250 (Present Value: $350,000)
Purchase Timing: November 2017
Ownership Structure: Olivia

Capital Growth p.a.	Yield p.a.
5.50%	5.50%

Area/Location Strategy/ies	Property Selection Strategy/ies
Changing Places/Changing Faces	Reliable and Durable
City Fling	Ugly Duckling
No Vacancies	The Shoulder Rider
The Wave Rider	Size Matters

Investment Property 3

Purchase Price: $457,436 (Present Value: $350,000)
Purchase Timing: May 2021
Ownership Structure: Olivia

Capital Growth p.a.	Yield p.a.
5.50%	5.50%

Area/Location Strategy/ies	Property Selection Strategy/ies
Changing Places/Changing Faces	Scarce Diamond
City Fling	The Shoulder Rider
No Vacancies	The Piggy Backer
The Wave Rider	Reliable and Durable

Investment Property 4

Purchase Price: $340,215 (Present Value: $250,000)
Purchase Timing: September 2023
Ownership Structure: Olivia

Capital Growth p.a.	Yield p.a.
4.50%	6.50%

Area/Location Strategy/ies	Property Selection Strategy/ies
No Vacancies	Reliable and Durable
The Boomtowners	Ugly Duckling
Non-Aspirers	The Shoulder Rider
The Wave Rider	The Piggy Backer

Given Olivia's single income and the way she has to balance her single parent budget, the investment action is slower than some of the other case studies. Olivia simply doesn't have the cash flow to be making quicker acquisitions, so the time between some purchases is longer. You can see this in the four years between the purchase of properties two and three, as follows.

Summary

Description	Target Purchase Price	Target Date	Target Growth	Target Yield
Investment Property 1	$475,000	May 2016	6.00%	5.00%
Investment Property 2	$369,250	Nov 2017	5.50%	5.50%
Investment Property 3	$457,436	May 2021	5.50%	5.50%
Investment Property 4	$340,215	Sep 2023	4.50%	6.50%

Below is the lending story associated with building this portfolio of properties:

Description	Loan Amount	As At	Monthly* Repayment	Loan Type
Mortgage	$120,000	April 2016	$460	Int Only
Loan for Property 1	$503,500	May 2016	$2,518	Int Only
Loan for Property 2	$391,405	Nov 2017	$1,957	Int Only
Loan for Property 3	$484,882	May 2021	$2,424	Int Only
Loan for Property 4	$360,628	Sept 2023	$1,803	Int Only

*We assume a 6% interest rate on each loan

Four investment properties is the target

This idea of four investment properties has been pretty consistent for the case studies, which just highlights you don't need to own 10+ properties to retire wealthy. In fact, it's completely wrong to think about a number of properties at all; the combined value and combined income you will be able to derive is what you should be thinking about.

Olivia's strategy is more of a focus on balance and cash flow assets, meaning higher yield again to compensate for the lower surplus income she has to use for investing.

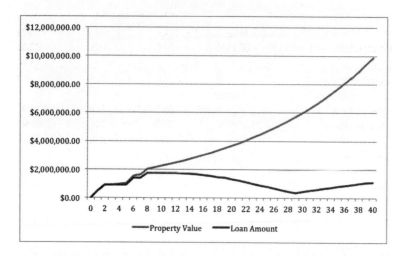

In the graph above you will notice that the debt actually hasn't been retired. In fact, the debt starts to increase after 28 years from today. What is happening here is that over time Olivia has been building up the surplus cash flows in an offset account and after retirement the $2,000 per week she is drawing in her self-funded retirement is reducing this balance and as it does the debt is going up.

Now you might wonder why Olivia wouldn't just sell some properties and pay out the debt. This is because she is now property- and money-wise. She understands how to control money and she understands where the wealth lies with property. If she sells them down, they won't add any more capital growth or rental income. If she can manage this money without selling any properties, those properties will go on to be worth more in the future and also generate greater rental income for her. And she will be able to pass on a very special legacy to Trudi, her daughter, and help set up the next generations of the family. A job well done we say!

| | | Financial Position at | | |
Description	Now 2016	10 Years 2026	20 Years 2036	Retirement 2038
Savings and Super	$172,000	$430,476	$970,511	$1,140,318
Investment Property	–	$2,242,116	$3,672,036	$4,184,797
Other Investments	–	–	–	–
Total Investment Assets	–	$2,242,116	$3,672,036	$4,184,797
Personal Assets	$680,000	$1,266,501	$2,358,859	$2,671,291
Total Assets	$852,000	$3,939,093	$7,001,406	$7,996,406
Total Debt	$92,000	$1,799,457	$1,319,751	$1,092,791
Net Worth	$760,000	$2,139,636	$5,681,655	$6,903,615
Nest-Egg (Investments)	$80,000	$873,136	$3,322,796	$4,232,324
Nest-Egg (In Present Value Terms)		$649,695	$1,839,752	$2,208,818

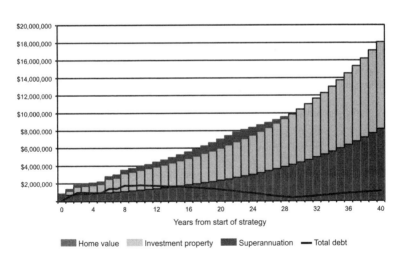

Years from start of strategy

Home value   Investment property   Superannuation   — Total debt

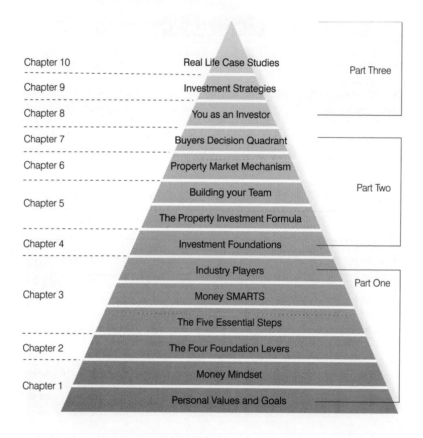

Chapter 10 — Real Life Case Studies — Part Three
Chapter 9 — Investment Strategies
Chapter 8 — You as an Investor
Chapter 7 — Buyers Decision Quadrant — Part Two
Chapter 6 — Property Market Mechanism
Chapter 5 — Building your Team / The Property Investment Formula
Chapter 4 — Investment Foundations
Industry Players — Part One
Chapter 3 — Money SMARTS
The Five Essential Steps
Chapter 2 — The Four Foundation Levers
Money Mindset
Chapter 1 — Personal Values and Goals

CONCLUSION

Congratulations on getting to this point – you have climbed to the top of the pyramid with a lot more knowledge about this whole property investing thing. Now your armchair ride can begin. However, just as with dieting, where nothing replaces eating well and regular exercise, so too it is with investing that nothing beats having a proven process and actioning it. We hope that reading this book gives you a great start on your investment journey. If you have already started, we hope we have given you a greater insight into all the important parts and that when put together they make for a very powerful result. Our wish is that you keep the book handy and use it as a constant resource that you refer to often.

Hopefully we've convinced you throughout this book that, whilst property investing is not easy, it is relatively simple when you follow a process and cover all the bases! There is nothing overly complicated about investing in property. Importantly, as you can see from our real world case studies, you don't have to be one of the chosen few on a high income or from a privileged background, who are afforded the exclusive opportunity at the expense of the majority, in order to achieve a comfortable retirement. Property investing does not discriminate against anyone and the barriers to entry are not too high. If you simply have the 'capacity', the 'intent' and finally a focused 'desire', then it is accessible to you.

Property investment advising doesn't need to be a zero-sum game. At the end of the day, there is a lot a money at play here and your financial future could be on the line. That's why we believe there is a place for ethical advisers to co-exist with helping their clients, where the adviser demonstrates value and the client actually receives that value and all egos are left at the door. This is an important message and I hope the pages you have just read have left you feeling confident and excited that you too can create your own passive income for retirement with residential real estate, but you don't have to do it alone if you don't want to.

Our final words: knowledge is 'empowering', but only if you act on it. Building passive income comes when the grunt work has been done – only then can you sit back and relax from your favourite armchair. Only one thing left to do… begin!

Over to you.

CONTACT US

If you'd like to know more about our company Empower Wealth or listen to our weekly podcast *The Property Couch – The Insider's Guide to Property Investing*, please visit **www.empowerwealth.com.au**, **www.thepropertycouch.com.au** or call **1300 123 842**.

We would love to receive your feedback on the book, please email us at: **armchairinvestor@thepropertycouch.com.au** and we will respond to you personally.

BONUS Content – We plan to continue to educate you with more case studies, videos and property investment content, so be sure to visit **www.thepropertycouch.com.au/armchairinvestor**.

INDEX

NOTES

NOTES

NOTES

NOTES

NOTES